The Gendered War

The Gendered War

Evaluating Feminist Ethnographic Narratives of the 1971 War of Bangladesh

Sanjib Kr Biswas and Priyanka Tripathi

BLOOMSBURY
NEW DELHI • LONDON • OXFORD • NEW YORK • SYDNEY

BLOOMSBURY INDIA
Bloomsbury Publishing India Pvt. Ltd
Second Floor, LSC Building No. 4, DDA Complex, Pocket C – 6 & 7,
Vasant Kunj, New Delhi, 110070

BLOOMSBURY, BLOOMSBURY ACADEMIC INDIA and the Diana logo
are trademarks of Bloomsbury Publishing Plc

First published in India 2023
This edition published 2023

Bloomsbury Academic India
An imprint of Bloomsbury Publishing Plc

ISBN: HB: 978-93-54359-01-9; eBook: 978-93-54359-57-6
2 4 6 8 10 9 7 5 3 1

For sale in the Indian subcontinent only

Typeset in Minion pro by Manipal Technologies Limited
Printed and bound in India by Replika Press Pvt. Ltd.

To find out more about our authors and books visit www.bloomsbury.com and sign up for our newsletters

Contents

Acknowledgements

This book has become possible with the help and support of many people and places connected to us, the first and foremost being the Department of Humanities and Social Sciences at the Indian Institute of Technology, Patna, for giving us the platform to conduct this research. Sanjib is very grateful to Professor Debabrata Paul (University of Calcutta, Kolkata) and Dr Prabir Roy for motivating him since his college days to undertake this research-oriented project. Professor Amrit Sen (Visva-Bharati University, Santiniketan) suggested books on the 1971 war, and Professor Pinaki Roy (Raiganj University, Raiganj) offered valuable suggestions and inputs whenever required. We are extremely indebted to Meghna Guhathakurta for sharing her memories of her father's martyrdom in the 1971 war. We are grateful to the people of Bangladesh and India, who voluntarily contributed their oral narratives related to their women's experiences in the 1971 war.

We are extremely thankful to the editors and publishers of *Journal of Gender Studies* (Routledge, United Kingdom), *Journal of International Women's Studies* (Bridgewater State University, United States of America), *Asiatic: IIUM Journal of English Language and Literature* (International Islamic University Malaysia) and *IUP Journal of English Studies*. We are thankful to Bloomsbury Publishing for finding merit and mojo in our manuscript and, especially, to Chandra Sekhar Ramachandruni, who was very supportive throughout this journey.

Finally, we are thankful to our family members! Without their support, this book would not have been possible.

1

Introduction: The Gendered History of the 1971 War and Women's Narratives

> The current historiography on the Liberation War is focused solely on the investigation and discussion of conflicts between the armies and militias of West Pakistan, East Pakistan, and India, and the external contexts of battles between the different ethnic groups of Bengalis, Biharis, and Pakistanis. The inner conflicts within the communities that led to rampant violence against women in the wars are overlooked and women's voices are actively silenced. As a result women's experiences and memories of the war are rendered invisible in the official history of 1971.
>
> —Yasmin Saikia, 'Beyond the Archive of Silence'

Introduction

War and violence have an inseparable connection that is well explored and documented in archives. However, in recent times, writers, ethnographers and critics have become conscious of the need to represent women in narratives. Female civilians have been sexually victimised in wars since ancient times whereas women who dare to participate actively in warfare and defence are overlooked in history and narratives (Cook 2006, xxvii). Women have not only been raped and killed in wars throughout the world but also been left to grieve over their dead sons and husbands who were brutally killed by enemies. Overall, the men regulating the war regime have seen women as subjects to be seized, raped, enslaved or left to live a miserable life (xxxi). Women left with bodily pain and the trauma of loss and violence are silenced within social discourses, and their representation in historiography bears hardly any connection to their real suffering. The process of silencing women's voices is not a new political phenomenon. Institutionalised sexism has been entrenched in society ever since the advent of civilisation with instances even in Western society where women are commonly perceived to have more access and, of course, more rights in their private, public and intellectual domains. Virginia Woolf (1882–1941), a pioneer of the feminist movement in the early 20th century, wrote about such gendered representation of women in history:

> History scarcely mentions her … The Crusades … The University … The House of Commons … The Hundred Years' War … The Wars of the Roses … The Renaissance Scholars … The Dissolution of the Monasteries … Agrarian and Religious Strife … The Origin of English Sea-power … The Armada … and so on. Occasionally an individual woman is mentioned, an Elizabeth, or a Mary; a queen or a great lady. But by no possible means could middle-class women with nothing but brains and character at their command have taken part in any one of the great movements which, brought together, constitute the historian's view of the past. ([1929] 1977, 37–38)

To bring women's real experiences in a war to the fore, recently, feminist ethnographic narratives have endeavoured to cover the untold stories of female fighters and victims in war. However, those narratives also suffer from a lack of accuracy and objectivity; the fabrication of the narratives has become a matter of concern. Feminist authors who have compiled the experiences of the women in their books can hardly get rid of the dominant 'great man' history (Barbre et al. 1989, 3). Starting with a premise that women have generally been sidelined from the pages of history, this book intends to reinvestigate the politics of representation of women, particularly in the war narratives of the Liberation War of Bangladesh of 1971. While locating women's roles in the Liberation War, two popular yet contradictory images occur to readers and critics: one is a photograph by Naibuddin Ahmed of a Birangona[1] with "'dishevelled hair', 'her loud laughter' and her 'quietness' or 'muteness'" (Mookherjee 2015b, xvi). The lives of the Birangona are divided between the loud laughter and muteness, both symbolising their unnatural mental condition. Naibuddin Ahmed's hair photograph has a storytelling quality that catches such glimpses of the lives of these women. Another image is the portrayal of Bangladeshi women as armed and courageous freedom fighters.[2] In both cases, the method of representation has built a twofold public memory about the women in the Liberation War: one is of the despised and raped, and another one is of the glorious contributor to the freedom movement of Bangladesh. The politics of representation has silenced those women's voices and denied their real experience as rape survivors, fighters, motivators, social workers, refugees, and glorified war heroines.

Stuart J. Hall focuses on the impact of representation on the formation of social and cultural consciousness among people and suggests that one of the most common aspects of representation is to say something meaningful or to represent something to the world meaningfully (1997, 15). According to Hall, meaning is always produced and exchanged among people of various cultures in the process of representation (15). He suggests that meaning is produced through representation via 'the reflective, the intentional and the constructionist' approach (15). Intentional and constructionist representations create a discursive image of something that is quite far apart from the real object. Hall says:

> If you put down a glass you are holding and walk out of the room, you can still think about the glass, even though it is no longer physically there. You can't think of a glass. You can only think about the concept of the glass. As the linguists are fond of saying 'Dogs bark, but the concept of "dog" cannot bark or bite'. (1997, 17)

Similarly, the representation of the concept of Birangona and other women activists of the Bangladesh Liberation War aligns with Hall's concept of a 'dog' that cannot protest against perpetrators of violence or defend against the politics of representation. The androcentric nature of war history misrepresents women who not only play humanitarian roles as nurses of wounded soldiers and the mothers of the disappeared but also take part in military action. Sometimes, their skill surpasses that of the male fighters (Karam 2000, 7). Only when the women's voices cross the barriers of public secrecy and State-sponsored silence do their actual survival stories become known. The noted postcolonial feminist Gayatri Chakravorty Spivak broadly discusses the role of the politics of representation in postcolonial historiography in bypassing women's voices. Citing Foucault, she vehemently argues, 'The oppressed, if given the chance (the problem of representation cannot be bypassed here), and on the way to solidarity through alliance politics (a Marxist thematic is at work here) can speak and know their conditions' (Spivak 1988, 25). Nayanika Mookherjee defends the voice of the oppressed in a tone similar to Spivak's. She says that the current historiography focusing on the lives of the Birangona does not document the real experience of the victims (Mookherjee 2015b, 14). After reinvestigating the lives of the rape survivors of the 1971 war, Yasmin Saikia affirms that they could tell their experiences of suffering and prejudices if the State and the society would allow them to do so (2004, 277).

To break the pervading silence of traditional historiography, this book aims to reinvestigate the role of women in making Bangladesh and analyse the plight of those women who faced the 1971 war in Bangladesh through the lens of feminist ethnographic narratives. The narrative is very important as a form in this research because it erases the boundary between specialised areas of knowledge like literature, anthropology, cultural studies, conflict studies and the like. There is a deep underlying connection between history and narratives. The term 'history' comes from the term *story* and 'stories are told' (Brüggemeier 1986, 6). Margaret Homans discusses why studies in narratives are so important in interdisciplinary studies and research. She cites an example in which an anthropologist represents a culture and celebrates storytelling by writing a novel titled *Their Eyes* (1994, 8). The narratives break the walls between fiction and creative non-fiction. Hence, they are an important form in human subject research, especially when the lives of victims and survivors are presented in writings. The narrative is a vital resource to present women's lives in writings. Feminist critics of the 20th century have endeavoured to create their narrative theory because they thought that the traditional narrative is from a male's perspective and, hence, has a gender bias (5). When feminist writers write their narratives, as suggested by Virginia Woolf, they break the sentence and sequence to create something new that reflects their lives well ([1929] 1977, 88). Creating a genre of feminist narratives is not an easy task because women's self-narratives are always influenced by the embedded gendered stories of society. Hence the process of 're-story' is crucial to bring their lives into narratives (Lee 1997, 2). If women want to create their historiography, the first thing they need to do is to overcome the politics of patriarchal representation. Postcolonial feminist theory is more accurate when talking about women's resistance against the politics of representation in the South Asian region because it contextualises women's issues instead of generalising them. Forging women of different countries as members of the single group 'women' provokes us to study the group based on a general notion of their subordination (Mohanty 1984, 344).

In the traditional historiography related to the birth of Bangladesh, women are presented merely as victims of the war and as statistics without any mention of their different roles and agencies in the war. The general belief is that 200,000–400,000 women were raped during the nine months of the freedom struggle (Linton 2010b, 194). To overcome the grip of gendered representation in history, this book aims to focus on women's roles as participants and survivors in the 1971 war through feminist narratives, both fictional and non-fictional. First, the position of women in the 1971 war of Bangladesh has been traced through a detailed study of the historical accounts. Some historical deeds that have been discussed are Zafar Iqbal's *Muktijuddher Itihas* (2008), the Bangladesh government's official publication *Bangladesher Shadhinota Juddha: Dolilpotro* ([1982] 2009), Srinath Raghavan's *1971: A Global History of the Creation of Bangladesh* (2013), Iftikhar Malik's *The History of Pakistan* (2008) and Willem van Schendel's *A History of Bangladesh* (2009). As this historical analysis is broad and occupies an important place in this research, it has been separated from the main literature review section, and the second chapter of the book has been dedicated to it. A detailed analysis of these historical texts shows that women's contribution to the making of Bangladesh has been largely ignored. Even the official deed of the Government of Bangladesh fails to recognise women's various roles in the freedom struggle as doctors, nurses, armed fighters and collaborators (Rahman [1982] 2009). So, the necessity for women's historiography is felt to bring the women's stories into focus. Due to the recent outcome of feminist narratives in the forms of fiction, oral testimony, interview, memoir and autobiography, the scope of writing lives has broadened. When history appears to be too gendered to interpret the truth objectively, these narratives might be a solution to the problem of representing the general human concern, a procedure to convert knowledge into tales (White 1980, 5). Feminist ethnographic narratives on the Liberation War of Bangladesh have interpreted the lives of the women against the backdrop of the war and its aftermath based on oral histories retrieved directly from their lives. The fictional narratives chosen for interpreting women's plights in the context of the 1971 war are Tahmima Anam's *A Golden Age* (2007), Dilruba Z. Ara's *Blame* (2015) and Kamila Shamsie's *Kartography* (2002). The non-fictional accounts chosen to depict the real-life experiences of the women are *Aami Birangona Balchi* by Neelima Ibrahim[3] (1994),[4] *Dead Reckoning: Memories of the 1971 Bangladesh War* by Sarmila Bose (2011a) and *Women, War, and the Making of Bangladesh: Remembering 1971* by Yasmin Saikia (2011b).

Besides these, we have looked at Nayanika Mookherjee's *The Spectral Wound: Sexual Violence, Public Memories, and the Bangladesh War of 1971* (2015b) for our study.

The 1971 War in Bangladesh: A Brief Overview

The Bangladesh Liberation War has gotten very little attention in world academia due to conflicting narratives and lack of resources. If the intensity of violence, the number of deaths and casualties and the nature of gendered violence are considered, the war of 1971 can be considered one of the most barbaric events that happened in the world. Ethnicity became the main issue behind the conflict, and the root of the 1971 war lies in the Partition of 1947. Pakistan was created based on the two-nation theory. Muslim-majority Pakistan was separated into two parts, East Pakistan on the eastern side of India and West Pakistan on the western side of India with a geographical distance of more than 2,000 kilometres between them. However, Muhammad Ali Jinnah's[5] two-nation theory did not account for East Pakistan's rich cultural heritage, and the people of East Pakistan thought that language and ethnicity, not religion, form the basis for a perfect nation. Many reasons were there for the outburst of the Bengali people against the Pakistan government. Bengalis constituted a very small portion of Pakistan's civil service, military service, police and other sectors (Rahman 2018). The trouble started mainly in 1948 when the Pakistan government tried to impose Urdu as the official language of both parts of Pakistan, even though more than 90 per cent of people in East Pakistan spoke Bengali. The revolt broke out when, on 27 January 1952, the then prime minister of Pakistan finally announced that only Urdu would be the national language of undivided Pakistan (Rahman 2018). The students of Dhaka Medical College and the University of Dhaka broke the protocol of the general curfew imposed and organised a mass protest for the right to their mother tongue, which came to be known as the Language

Movement.[6] Police attacked the students and mercilessly shot many, such as Barkat, Rafiq, Jabbar, Shafiur and Salam, to death. Their sacrifice for their language later received international recognition, and 21 February is celebrated as International Mother Language Day throughout the world since the declaration by the United Nations Educational, Scientific and Cultural Organization (UNESCO) in 1999 (Rahman 2018).

Bengalis[7] got the right to speak in Bengali, but the discrimination and prejudices continued. Due to the vast geographical distance and major ethnic differences, it was very problematic for Pakistan to be united based solely on religion (Iqbal 2008, 1–2). East Pakistan was a major jute-producing area and earned a significant portion of Pakistan's revenue. Despite this, the eastern wing received very limited resources to establish schools, hospitals, roads, infrastructure and so on. Sheikh Mujibur Rahman[8] emerged as an uncompromising leader at this time, and his six-point demands created a major impact on Pakistani government. Due to prolonged economic and social disparity, Mujib issued an ultimatum and presented six-point demands, which included the demands for a federal constitution in Pakistan, separate currencies in the east and west wings, safeguards against the flight of funds from East Pakistan to West Pakistan, autonomous power of taxation and revenue collection, separate foreign exchange account and self-sufficiency in defence (Ranjan 2016, 3). The deprived citizens of East Pakistan, led by Mujib, demanded the transfer of power based on the result of Pakistan's 1970 general election. In the 1970 election, Mujib's party secured a massive victory in East Pakistan, and they demanded the right to form a government in the region. After the victory, Mujib was not given the opportunity to form a government, and the people of Bangladesh became enraged. When the spirit of the freedom struggle was high, Sheikh Mujibur Rahman's speech on 7 March 1971 at the Dhaka Racecourse Ground inspired the people to fight against Pakistanis with everything they had. Mujib urged the citizens, 'Our struggle this time is a struggle for freedom. Our struggle this time is a struggle for independence. Joi Bangla' (Ara 2015, 167). To control the rebellion, Yahya Khan[9] and his close associate Zulfikar Ali Bhutto[10] flew to East Pakistan. They resorted to violence and atrocities without providing East Pakistan with the rights they deserved. On 25 March 1971, a mission led by Yahya Khan, 'Operation Searchlight', was initiated in East Pakistan to kill Bengali intellectuals and civilians in mass numbers (Iqbal 2008, 7). During this time, the Pakistani government aimed to curb Mujib's power. He was arrested on 26 March 1971. Before being arrested, Mujib declared the independence of Bangladesh and asked the people to free their country at any cost from the Pakistanis. The people of Bangladesh formed the Muktibahini[11] and participated in the war in large numbers, even without proper training and modern arms initially. So, the number of deaths and casualties increased. India helped Bangladesh from the beginning of the war. On 27 March 1971, Indira Gandhi[12] declared all possible help for Bangladesh and opened all Indo-Bangladesh borders to shelter millions of refugees. Training camps were established in West Bengal, Tripura, Assam, Meghalaya and Bihar to train Bengali army officials and freedom fighters (Andrio 2016, 737). Due to India's support, Bangladesh was able to cope with the situation and achieved victory over Pakistan on 16 December 1971. In the meantime, the nine-month freedom struggle had caused a lot of casualties and gendered violence. According to Bangladesh's estimate, the number of deaths crossed three million, though Pakistani sources claim 26,000 deaths (Linton 2010b, 194, 202). One of the cruellest sides of the war is the gendered crimes by Pakistani perpetrators and Bengali collaborators known as Razakars[13]. Though there is a discrepancy between the number of victims in the narratives of Bangladesh and Pakistan, the general estimate from Bangladesh's side is that approximately 200,000 to 400,000 women were raped, followed by the pregnancy of more than 25,000 women (Linton 2010b, 194).

In 1972, the rape survivors of Bangladesh were honoured by the Government of Bangladesh with the title of 'Birangona', and they were rehabilitated with shelter, education, and work opportunities (Mookherjee 2006, 432, 436).

Women and War

Since its origin, literature has had a deep-rooted connection with the history of war. Throughout the ages, mythological and historical wars were the backdrops of works by writers such as Homer, Sophocles, Kalidasa, Chaucer, Shakespeare, T.S. Eliot and so on. *War and Literature*, edited by Laura Ashe and Ian Patterson, deals with the contingent roles between war and literature in almost chronological order, focusing on how wars have contributed to plots and themes in literature since its origin (2014). 'War was the first subject of literature; at times, war has been its only subject', the editors say in the preface (Ashe and Patterson 2014, xi). Susanna A. Throop's chapter in the book focuses on how secular and spiritual vengeance are subjects of religious literature (2014, 7). Carol Watts presents some women's experiences during the Second World War, showing how women and children were kept in safe custody during troubled times. She also focuses on Hannah Arendt, Emily Dickinson and some other writers who penned the stories of apprenticed women soldiers (2014, 142). In the 20th century, women's representation in war history and war literature became a vital topic of academic research. Bernard A. Cook's historical encyclopedia is broadly about women's agency and victimhood in wartime in different global contexts (2006). Cook's encyclopedia sorts women based on their roles and engagement in world conflicts as armed fighters, caregivers and policy makers as well as raped, tortured, killed and stigmatised people. The foreword to the book mentions that history is completely gendered and a men's domain where women's active contributions and traditional roles in wars have largely been ignored (Cook 2006, xxvii). Cook asserts that throughout history, women have significantly involved themselves in wars to fight and resist threats to save their tribes, villages and towns (xxxi). Referring to Queen Boudicca of Britain and Queen Durgawati of India, Cook confirms that women came to the warfront and replaced their brothers, husbands or fathers after they were wounded or killed (xxxi). In an ethnic struggle, women are singled out for atrocities because they are considered to be the bearers of a nation (xxxi). Among the modes of violence initiated against women in an ethnic struggle, rape, according to Cook, is the most common. He presents a series of ethnic conflicts that happened in Bangladesh, Cambodia, Haiti, Liberia, Rwanda, Indonesia, Serbia and Uganda where rape was used as a weapon to degrade the enemies physically and psychologically (481–482). The account of *comfort women* during the Second World War in Cook's book gives us a clear image of how women have been used as puppets in the hands of men. These 200,000 comfort women, who were mainly Korean, were used as sex slaves by the Japanese military. Three-quarters of them died during the war, and the rest of them suffered malnourishment and developed severe physical and psychological disorders after the war (347). Cook's book contributes a lot to exploring women's plights in wars, their untold stories of participation in the armed conflicts as soldiers and their victimisation in ethnic conflicts through rape.

Women played different significant roles not only during the war but also in the peace process. Azza Karam's article examines women's active roles during war and post-conflict resolutions (2000). The author painfully observes that the patriarchal structure of society fixes women's positions in war literature; they are represented mostly as victims rather than active participants (Karam 2000, 2). Though war is always thought of as a men's game, women actively contributed as armed fighters in conflicts and peacemaking processes (2). The author emphasises the participation of women during hard times: 'Women form an essential half of any society, even in conflict' (2). The article begins by defining war and conflict as interstate and intrastate armed struggles respectively. Women's lives are shown to have been reshaped during the civil wars in Sri Lanka, Iraq, Afghanistan, Palestine and Bosnia due to the loss of their dear ones and property (4). Women in conflict-prone zones like El Salvador, Guatemala and Sri Lanka receive fewer resources and opportunities from their governments as those respective countries spend heavily on their armed forces (4). Sri Lanka, Yugoslavia and Israel have recorded an increase in domestic violence against women in parallel to the increase in atrocities in societies due to war (5). Wartime prostitution was frequent during the Second World War when the Korean women were termed as 'comfort women' by the Japanese army (5–6). Karam discusses a few recent studies on the androcentric nature of war that results in a male-dominated culture in soldiering (6). In reality, women play multifaceted roles as caregivers, nurses, armed fighters and even policy makers in the wars (7). In post-conflict times, tagging women just as victims and discussing their suffering only impose a limit on women's roles in the war (7). Citing Meredeth Turshen, Karam writes that war sometimes breaks the patriarchal structure in the society and provides an opportunity for women to gain positive gender relationships and access ownership of property, such as in Chad, Rwanda and Mozambique (8). She refers to the post-conflict situations in countries like Afghanistan, Uganda, Cambodia, Liberia and Guatemala where women played significant roles in serious affairs like peace talks and the drafting of their national constitutions (14–15). Throughout the 20th century, women's participation was sought in the national liberation struggles of many countries, and the liberation of those countries also brought liberation for women (17). In the concluding section of the essay, Karam challenges the historians and the writers of the age to represent the deeds of women in conflicts and conflict resolution processes with 'specialized attention' (18). The author tries to resolve the problem of representing women in a few points: extending academic studies on war and women, stopping misrepresentation of women as just victims in popular media, addressing women's situations in armed conflicts and peace and so on (18–20).

The end of the war in a country signifies men's freedom from political bondage but hardly ensures women's freedom from oppression and prejudices. Sheila Meintjes's article shows how the end of conflicts in many countries is followed by increased violence towards women by their male counterparts (2000). The author has researched the post-war social conditions of different Third World[14] African and Asian countries and found one thing almost common: during the transitional period of peacemaking, women experience violence as 'normal or cultural facts' (Meintjes 2000, 4). Even women who were great fighters, peacemakers and mothers during the conflicts face gang rape, mass killing and severe physical and mental threats once the conflicts end (4). Men are still directed to cherish their newly gained spirit of tormenting others. The patriarchy-based social structure in South Asian nations like India, Pakistan and Bangladesh is suitable for their men to initiate domestic violence towards their women. When they become habituated to exhibiting their masculinity during the time of conflict, they can hardly get rid of the hyper-masculine idea of tormenting the weaker sections of society in peacetime. Women become the first-hand victims of the men's changed mentality because patriarchy has turned them into the weaker sex with no or very limited work opportunity and academic exposure. The economic dependency of women in South Asian countries like Sri Lanka leads them to tolerate the abuse without any protest. Meintjes's article follows a series of discussions, one of them being the tendency to blame the victims. The author says that a similar experience is faced by women all across the world where they are blamed for their victimisation despite having no hand in it (6). Then the author discusses women's victimisation through rape in different African countries like Rwanda and Haiti and the treatment of wartime rape in African culture. In Haiti, rape is considered not a crime of violence but a crime of honour or passion. Hence, a rapist escapes punishment by marrying the victim (7). A major portion of Meintjes's article deals with gender identities and gender roles among men and women during the peak time of conflict. Women still conform to their traditional gender roles during the war because they need to take care of their house and children. On the other hand, men's ability and sense of masculinity are attacked and humiliated by their enemies. They experience shame and humiliation when their enemies rape their mothers, wives or daughters in front of them (8). Rape not only mentally and physically tortures the victims but also threatens the community by bringing shame to the men who could not protect their women and children (8).

Women of the 1971 War in Postcolonial Writings

While Western feminists seem to be ignorant about women's agency in wars in the South Asian context, the end of the 20th century and the beginning of the 21st century saw many such academic works published in South Asia. Aparna Sundar and Nandini Sundar's work is a chronological study of the causes and consequences of civil wars in South Asia (2014). Their book is a collection of essays that focus on how South Asia has become a prospective zone for the studies and research of civil wars and insurgencies. The authors present their arguments with special reference to the ethnic conflicts in Kashmir and the North East of India and the ongoing armed conflicts in Pakistan and Afghanistan. However, we intend to do a close reading of the portion that discusses the passion for ethnic identity over the religious one, a cause that led the Bengali nationalists to form Bangladesh and separate from their second colonial master, Pakistan. The Liberation War of Bangladesh or 'a classic civil war with internal roots' has been prioritised in Sundar and Sundar's book (2014, 44). Considerable factual and figurative information has been provided about ethnic crimes committed through rape and genocide by Pakistanis, Biharis[15] and Bangladeshis. The writers acknowledge the conflicting number of casualties in the war. As per Bangladesh's claim, three million were killed, and 200,000 women were raped, whereas the official declaration of Pakistan only acknowledges 26,000 deaths (44). Aparna and Nandini have measured the ethnic struggles of Bangladesh and Kashmir with the same parameter in some cases because both areas became engaged in internal conflicts as soon as they were exposed to the 'postcolonial boundary' (46). While discussing women in the context of the ethnic conflicts in South Asia, the writers say that men and women have different experiences in wartime. The plight of the Birangona in Bangladesh shows that women remain stigmatised even when they are on the victorious side (46).

Academic writings that present gender issues in South Asian contexts have focused on the 1971 war in Bangladesh because of the intensity of gendered violence that took place. Bina D'Costa's groundbreaking ethnographic work explores how gendered violence and war crimes have become associated with the formation of the nation in South Asia (2011). The author mainly focuses on two conflicts in South Asia: the Partition of 1947 and the Liberation War of Bangladesh of 1971. However, the 1971 war has been prioritised in D'Costa's writing. The author has asked the writers and thinkers of the age to reinvestigate the war crimes of 1971 and explore the issues of gendered violence that have largely been neglected in the national narratives of Bangladesh. D'Costa starts by stating that the feminist literature of the Global South has been quite influenced by the nationalism-based feminist literature of the Global North. The latter provides 'both valuable insight and an analytical point of departure for scholars of the South, for whom experience of colonialism, discrimination, suppression of rights and various kinds of structural violence (such as poverty and patriarchy) have shaped the understanding of gender' (D'Costa 2011, 9). The misconceptions and ignorance of Western feminist scholars towards the East continues through their writings, which have given very little priority to the role of women of South Asia in the process of nation-building.

The experience of the women of the 1971 war has almost remained untouched by academicians in their discussion of nationalism and nation-building (9). D'Costa's book has a total of six contributory chapters apart from the introduction and the conclusion, and the appendix section includes two interviews by D'Costa with activists who had direct dealings with the victims of the war. The third chapter, titled '1971: The Politics of Silence or Refusal to Remember?', provides a detailed demographic presentation of East Pakistan and the territorial, economic, cultural and political factors behind the separation of East Pakistan and the creation of Bangladesh (76–109). The next chapter, 'Gendered Nationbuilding', is a detailed study of victims of sexual assault, their recognition as Birangona by Mujib, abortions, war babies, narratives in Bangladeshi newspapers and Neelima Ibrahim's books, Hindu women as special targets and, finally, the denial of women's identities as war heroes despite their worthy contribution to the freedom struggle (110–143). The second interview in the appendix section with Dr Geoffrey Davis is crucial to know the condition of the Birangona of Bangladesh in the postcolonial age (194–200). Davis, a medical graduate from Sydney, was appointed to the abortion and rehabilitation process of the rape survivors in Bangladesh in 1972, and his declaration clarifies many doubts about the number of women who were raped and their position in society. Dr Davis dismisses Pakistan's claims of exaggeration of the number of women who experienced sexual violence. According to him, the actual number is much higher (197).

The Birangona's role in the birth of Bangladesh has got an important place in the academic writings of Nayanika Mookherjee, an Indian writer and an associate professor of anthropology at Durham University, United Kingdom. Her paper recounts the victimisation of women in 1971 and their problems in today's Bangladesh (Mookherjee 2006). 'Birangona' is a title that was conferred on all the rape survivors of the 1971 war by the Bangladesh government in 1972 to save them from social stigmatisation and to rehabilitate them through employment and marriage (432, 436). Mookherjee broadly examines the dualities between being Birangona (the brave heroine of the war) and being rape victims tolerating continuous *khota*s (sarcastic remarks referring to an unpleasant event) (432). She starts her article with a reference to three Liberation War rape survivors whose photo was printed on the front page of a Bangladeshi national newspaper due to their bravery in seeking the trial of Ghulam Azam, one of the Bengali collaborators of the Pakistanis in 1971. Mookherjee's article is divided into three sections: the first section locates the three women in the contemporary historical and political context of Bangladesh. The second section focuses on the meaning of the term *khota* at Enayetpur (a village in western Bangladesh) and its relation to public secrecy, female sexuality and the female body. The third section contains the narratives of the 'remembrance of 1971 and examines the process of revelation and concealment' (435). Mookherjee moves back to 1990s Bangladesh when the narratives of rape survivors suddenly became critical for two reasons: first, in 1992, *Gono Adalat* (people's tribunal), led by political and cultural activists such as Jahanara Imam, sought the trials of the Pakistani collaborators like Ghulam Azam, and second, the International Crimes Tribunal of Bangladesh recognised rape as a war crime (436). Mookherjee shows how the knowledge of rape is a matter of public secrecy in countries like Bangladesh where women are thought to be bearers of shame when their victimisation at the hands of enemies is exposed publicly. Rape is even linked with prostitution. The people of Enayetpur refer to those women as sinners for bringing up their narratives of victimisation after breaking a prolonged silence (438–439). Mookherjee observes with pain that local liberation warfighters do not equate the courageous deeds and survival of the Birangona with their heroism (441). She concludes her essay with an assertion that people 'remember to forget', referring to the secrecy of rape. Hence, the villagers apply *khota* to the women, which hides everything associated with rape in women's lives (446).

Mookherjee's next article provides insights into the postcolonial social status of the wartime rape victims of Bangladesh through their survival stories and photographs (2015a). She shows that the public memory of wartime rape is influenced by the aesthetical representation of the Birangona through narratives and photographs (379). Mookherjee starts her discussion by quoting a play director who was going to direct a play on the Birangona based on the testimonies from a group of Birangona. Based on her father's account, the director tells Mookherjee that after the 1971 war, hundreds of Birangona were seen in the streets of Dhaka back to back in a convoy of trucks. They were mute and traumatised like sacrificial animals (379–380). Such representations are similar to Naibuddin Ahmed's 'hair photograph' (1998) of the Birangona. Ahmed's photograph of the Birangona with 'dishevelled hair', 'loud laughter' and 'muteness' gives an insight into the nature of their representation in popular culture (381). Apart from the real accounts of the sufferings of the Birangona, people are more interested in various narratives of them staying with enemies during the war followed by their pregnancy and shameful life in exile (381). Mookherjee then gives details about the photograph by Naibuddin Ahmed. According to Tahmima Anam, it is one of the most haunting photos representing Bangladesh in 1971 (382). Shame, social prejudice, hatred and religious orthodoxy have turned the literal brave heroine mute and indifferent, like cattle, in post-war Bangladesh. Mookherjee cites Ranciere to show that the politics of representation is an aesthetic activity that leads to the formation of subjects (383). Since the end of the war, followed by the recognition of the survivors of sexual violence as Birangona, the women have become a source of literary and visual representation in Bangladesh (383–384). Academicians, the Bangladeshi press, feminist activists and filmmakers have recently portrayed them based on oral history, which is a new genre to present victims' narratives (384). The rape is considered a *bhoyonkor* (dreadful) event in Bangladesh, and the 'hair' photograph exhibits the intensity of such dreadfulness (386).

Mookherjee concludes her essay with a remark that such aesthetic representation tells us about the trauma of rape in the 1971 war and, at the same time, restrains us from studying the reality of the lives of Birangona in the post-war context (393).

Bihari women's victimisation by Bengali nationalists, an ignored side of gendered violence in the 1971 war, is discussed poignantly in many articles by Yasmin Saikia, an Indian writer currently working as a professor of history at the Arizona State University, United States of America. Saikia's article starts with an argument that in 1971, violence erupted in East Pakistan (now Bangladesh) because the West Pakistani military force and India became engaged in a two-dimensional war: a civil war between East and West Pakistan and an international war between India and Pakistan ((2004, 275). The author says that the civilians and the women living in East Pakistan were targeted in both cases (275). Saikia broadly focuses on the historical aspects of the migration of many Urdu-speaking people into East Pakistan after the Partition, and most of them supported the West Pakistani military force because of the ethnic connection (275). The Muktibahini, which was formed by the local Bengali nationalists, ensured their victory in the war after they received patronage from India (275). Saikia says that the present historiography only focuses on such outer conflicts based on ethnic issues, but the inner struggle in domestic and social life, experienced mostly by the women of the country, has been neglected (275). The author shares her experience of interviewing people of Bangladesh, India and Pakistan to reinvestigate the true story of the sexual violence in and after the 1971 war. She asserts that the roles and positions of women in the war are ignored, and the present one-sided historiography only shows Pakistanis as 'evil' and Bangladeshis as 'good', along with an extreme glorification of the Muktibahini (277). Saikia expresses her grief over the institutional silence of the country on women's issues and her belief that the survivors could speak if they were allowed to do so (277). She interviews both Bihari and Bengali women and other people who were active and passive observers of the sexual victimisation of a large number of women.

Saikia has documented many unknown and horrific stories of women's victimisation by Bengali nationalists. Importantly, there are accounts of the victimisation of an unnamed school teacher (279) and a Hindu girl (281) by their Bengali neighbours. Saikia records the narratives of many Bihari women who were raped by Bengali nationalists as revenge. She says, 'Driven by the spirit of nationalism and nation-building, these men committed horrific crimes that haunt them even today' (286).

After the end of the war, the lives of female survivors of the war are not happy. Though the 1971 war still has a strong impact on Bangladeshi politics, public consciousness and popular culture, the society is still prejudiced against them. T.M. Murshed discusses Bangladeshi women's power of resistance despite being subject to social, religious and political subordination (1997). He discusses the rehabilitation of the rape survivors or the Birangona after the war by the Bangladeshi government as an initial step to glorify the women who made sacrifices for the formation of the nation (120). The author goes on to discuss the subjugation of women under the governments led by former Bangladeshi presidents Major Ziaur Rahman[16] and Hussain Muhammad Ershad[17] after the political assassination of the founder prime minister of Bangladesh, Sheikh Mujibur Rahman, in 1975 (121). He discusses the survival of Bangladeshi women under the Islamic code of conduct after Bangladesh declared Islam as the official religion in their constitution in 1988. Dowry deaths, marriage, divorce and the like are not judged by the state law in most cases, and women face inequality while such disputes are being resolved under family laws (125). The author avers that the judicial system of postcolonial Bangladesh has become ineffective due to the attitude of the *fatwa* court, which announced the death verdict of Taslima Nasrin, a feminist activist and writer of Bangladeshi origin (126). The domination of the patriarchal social system and the fundamentalism of the people are the main hindrances to women's empowerment in postcolonial Bangladesh. Murshed says in his concluding remarks that postcolonial Bangladesh has become a weak mediator between the rigid social structure and the freedom of women (134).

The post-conflict plight of women in Bangladesh is also discussed in Saikia's article (2011a). Saikia expands on the concept of *insaniyat* or the sense of humanity felt by the victims and the perpetrators. She wonders if the understanding of humanity is different for the victims and the perpetrators in Bangladesh and Pakistan (475). The author starts by saying that the world has experienced much bloodshed and violence in the 20th century due to the unethical use of arms and the objectification of human beings (475–476). According to Saikia, as Bangladesh and Pakistan are both Muslim-majority countries, they can restore peace in their countries by following Indo-Islamic vocabularies, a way to heal from trauma that is based on religious and cultural understanding (476). The author thinks that the *insaniyat* of the perpetrators of violence and the victims would allow a solution for the eternal conflict in a non-violent way. The perpetrator would repent and apologise to the victims. On the other hand, the victims' forgiveness of the perpetrators, instead of seeking punishment for them, ends the cycle of violence (477). Saikia says that the postcolonial history of South Asia deprives people of their true identity and doesn't allow them to know who they are. Instead, it teaches them that they are Indian, Bangladeshi and Pakistani, enemies to each other (480–481). She writes that through a sense of humanity and the restoration of human rights, Bangladesh and Pakistan can free themselves from the trauma of the past and write the narratives of the 1971 war based on their mutual understanding (477–478). With very few women's narratives, Saikia is able to show how this kind of enmity among people of different ethnic classes led them to commit rape and genocide against the other community. The article recounts the survival stories of a few rape survivors, such as Aparna, a Bengali Hindu girl who lives in deplorable conditions in Bangladesh after the conflict ended. Having lost her relatives and suffering from trauma, Aparna became paralysed, and according to her, no one has come to rescue her in the last thirty years (487). Saikia also depicts Bihari women's dehumanisation in the camps in independent Bangladesh and their mental and physical survival like animals. She emphasises that women, irrespective of their ethnicity, were harassed, raped and used by the militants as well as by their men as per their motives during and after the war. Saikia claims that women like Aparna do not want revenge but need recognition, work opportunities and a means of living. She urges everyone to listen to the real survivors instead of yielding to political or religious agendas based on the narratives of their sufferings (496).

The war of 1971 had a significant impact on the politics of South Asia and led to restlessness in the relationship between India and Pakistan. Amit Ranjan writes about the conflicting roles of Pakistanis and Indians in the war narratives of the Bangladesh Liberation War in his article (2016). Ranjan has used the document of the Government of Bangladesh on the 1971 war, *Bangladesher Shadhinota Juddha: Dolilpotro*, as a primary source in his article (2). He questions why Bangladesh's politics is still regulated by the narratives of the 1971 war (1). He then discusses Bangladesh's pre-independence sociopolitical scenario and the economic disparity East Pakistan faced. Sheikh Mujibur Rahman's six-point list of demands, which included the demands for a federal government, a separate currency in East Pakistan, autonomy in tax and revenue collection and self-sufficiency in the matter of defence, were issued in 1967 due to that prolonged economic disparity (3). Ranjan takes into account how the Bengali culture became a dominating factor in the conflict from the 1950s to the 1970s in Pakistan. During the liberation war, the Bengali dress code of saree, *lal tip* (red dot worn on the forehead), Rabindra Sangeet and the like became the identification marks of Bengali ethnicity and Bengali nationalism that offended Pakistani leaders such as Yahya Khan (2–3). Ranjan cites Anthony Mascarenhas to write about the non-Bengali people (especially migrated Biharis) who also faced savagery during the war. Many women were raped, and their breasts were cut with special knives. The death toll of non-Bengali people may have been as high as 100,000 (5). In the section 'Impact of 1971 on Present', Ranjan mainly focuses on the Bihari people stranded in several camps in Bangladesh. Citing Khalid Hussain, Ranjan claims that Urdu-speaking Biharis are the most unfortunate people because they consider Bangladesh as their home but do not have citizenship (6). The author thinks that the 1971 war still determines the relationship between India and Pakistan. Pakistan still blames India for its role in the creation of Bangladesh (7–8). According to Ranjan, the war narratives of the nation still need to be verified, and the roles of Pakistan and India in the war should be reinvestigated. He talks about the recent trials of criminals that led a majority of the population in Bangladesh to express hatred and anger against the present judicial system that only focuses on a single side of the war (9). The author cites Sarmila Bose and David Bergmann and questions the inconsistency in the numbers of deaths and raped women in the genocide (11). Overall, this article broadly focuses on the recent research in South Asia on the 1971 genocide to show that the crimes against humanity were committed by the winning side too.

Feminist Narratives and Gendered History

One important aspect of this book is to have an interdisciplinary approach to history and narratives in the context of the 1971 war. F.J. Brüggemeier's article shows the basic similarities and dissimilarities between history, narrative and historiography (1986). Though they are thought to be contrasting ideas from their literal meanings, the author claims that history owes its root to story or narrative (Brüggemeier 1986, 6). According to the author, modern historians criticise the ancient model of presenting history without theory. He suggests that the sociological model should be preferred, with theoretical and methodological deliberation in history (6). The author refers to theorists like Danto and Baumgartner to state that theory holds the second position whereas explanation of any historical deed depends on the respective narratives (7).

Brüggemeier asserts that oral history, mainly in the form of interviews, gives a vital narrative concept in the studies of historical deeds as people can speak for themselves (8). Through oral history, the subalterns can speak for themselves because it helps them to present their voice beyond any type of political representation. Gayatri Chakraborty Spivak's article is a groundbreaking work in the studies of subalternity (1988). Spivak cites Foucault and Deleuze to impart her primary notion of the subaltern voice. She asserts that the subaltern can speak if they can bypass the problem of representation (Spivak 1998, 25). She primarily refers to Ranajit Guha's works on subalternity and colonial historiography. According to her proposition, the history of India's nationalism has long been dominated by two types of elitism: colonist elitism and bourgeois-nationalist elitism (25). Such dominance not only avoided the voice of the marginalised class but also made women more marginalised in history. The ideological construction of gender has ensured male dominance in colonist historiography despite women's proven roles in war and insurgency. If history continues to remain such a colonial production, the subaltern has no voice, and women as a subaltern class are more victimised (28).

The emergence of oral history in books and newspapers has ensured that the women of the 1971 war left their subaltern position. Aasha Mehreen Amin, Lavina Ambreen Ahmed and Shamim Ahsan discuss the gendered nature of the war history of Bangladesh and the way to retrieve the position of women in the pages of history and public consciousness in their newspaper article (2016). The authors acknowledge that the greatest shortcoming of the nation in its dealing with the Liberation War is Bangladesh's failure to recognise the role of women. The reason for this failure is a popular belief that war is only a matter of weapons and physical power. The authors redefine the concept of a war hero. Generally, in Bangladesh, *Muktijoddhas* or male freedom fighters are adored as war heroes, while women who gave up their dear ones or fought in the war are not included in this category. The official documents of the Bangladeshi freedom struggle mention the names of many male freedom fighters. Women like Taramon Bibi, who fought in the 1971 war in Sector 11 of Bangladesh and was awarded 'Bir Pratik' (an honorary title for freedom fighters), are hardly mentioned (Amin et al. 2016). Taramon Bibi did no less than her associate male freedom fighters. Her memoir speaks of the commitment she possessed: 'We were fighting to free our country ... the last thing on my mind was worrying about my own safety' (Amin et al. 2016). Taramon, who escaped death in 1971, now lives with her former husband in poverty and without any recognition. She expresses her grief to the authors that the government gave money and other benefits to male freedom fighters, but she gained nothing because a female freedom fighter is never taken seriously. Dr Captain Sitara Begum is another lady who got the Bir Pratik award from the Government of Bangladesh. She received a medical degree from Dhaka Medical College in 1970 and joined the freedom struggle of Bangladesh in the turbulent times of the country. Later, Sitara served the wounded soldiers and Bangladeshi refugees in a hospital in Meghalaya, India, where she heard about Bangladesh's victory on 16 December on the radio. Another valiant soldier, Gita Kar, joined a group of 200 female guerrilla fighters to free the country from Pakistan's atrocities. Later, she served as an attendant in a hospital in Agartala, India, that offered treatment to wounded freedom fighters. Women such as Rabeya and Rokeya Begum also came to the warfront to free the nation, and they never lost their courage even after losing their dear ones in battle. Unfortunately, however, their stories of courage, bravery and survival got hardly any place in the State-sponsored historiography. The writers conclude in a way that respects the contribution of these women during the war and in its aftermath:

> Whether they find room in the pages of history or not, it is an undeniable truth that it was their sacrifice and strength that helped us to win our freedom. For these poor, ordinary village women who had

> to fight simultaneous enemies on a personal, social, and national level, the fight goes on. (Amin et al. 2016)

Ethnographic methodology, in general, and feminist ethnography, in particular, help a researcher to trace the plight of women in/beyond an ethnic group. Feminist ethnography as a methodology helps the researcher to align his or her research to come out of the rigid and restricted sphere of feminism through an anthropological intervention. Kristin Aune defines 'feminist ethnography' as a methodology of research conducted over time (2009, 309). The research originates from a commitment to women to look into gender issues across society (309). She also discusses the gradual shift of feminist ethnography as a research methodology since 1970s to understand it as diverse written constructions of gendered experiences (309). Before interrogating if feminist ethnography is possible, Aune traces the roots of the ethnography methodology developed by sociologists and adopted by anthropologists through observing the lives of a group as an insider as well as an outsider, resulting in the 'product' or the written account of the research after the completion of fieldwork (309). In its earlier form, feminist ethnography challenged the marginalisation of women and the tendency to avoid the representation of women's experience and sought to give a voice to the voiceless (310). There was a turn in the 1980s and 1990s when feminist ethnographers started to focus on the power structure created by men and masculinity (309–312). After the advent of postmodernism, feminist ethnography shifted its focus more prominently to 'diversity, representation and symbolic realm' (311). Kristine Aune emphasises the contribution of women researchers in the feminist ethnographic research for several reasons. According to her, researchers who are women are more able to create successful relations with a group of women in a community. They experience less opposition because they do not seem threatening or authoritative to a community (311). With a variety of genres like poetry, diary writing, linear narratives or fiction, letters, photography and so on, the postmodern approach to ethnography promotes various types of voices in a single issue but never claims to settle the truth (313). Aune concludes her essay by determining the possibility of feminist ethnography as a methodology to give women a voice, one that has been denied to them for decades. She writes, 'In representing and constructing the lives of their participants, feminist ethnographers try to move beyond the dichotomies of victimhood or agency, recognizing that choice and constraint are intertwined in women's lives' (314).

Feminist ethnography goes hand in hand with postcolonial feminism, but it is a broader concept. While postcolonial feminism only seeks to engage women of the same region and its diaspora to derive women's issues, feminist ethnography advocates a context-specific pluralistic study of women and avoids the concept of women as a universal category. Dána-Ain Davis and Christa Craven discuss the relation and contradiction between the traditional feminist method and feminist ethnography in their book (2016). According to Davis and Craven, feminist ethnography as a term and a methodology is very important to defend feminism in recent times because it has gained a negative connotation with time. After the introduction of the third wave of feminism in the 1990s, feminism has been associated with antiracism, anticolonialism, queer rights, reproductive rights and so on. Hence, feminism faced public resistance in the conservative political environment of the 1980s and 1990s (Davis and Craven 2016, 1). Sanjukta Ghosh creates a link between ethnography and feminist ethnography and interrogates the relevance of feminist ethnography as an emerging research methodology in her article (2016). Ghosh defines ethnography as an analytical technique that allows a researcher to collect data on the culture of a community mainly through two processes: participant observation and interviews (2016, 1). Ethnography helps feminist researchers foreground their knowledge based on 'lived experience' and 'concrete realities' of people's lives, and it endeavours to allow a voice to the subjects (2). Derived from anthropology, feminist ethnography is a qualitative research method that studies the experience of a community in its natural living place (1).

Feminist ethnography constitutes a free method to study gender issues beyond the 'androcentric' and 'Eurocentric' perspectives (1). The third period and the present mode of feminist ethnography began in the 1980s with greater attention to discourse deriving theoretical ideas from post-structuralism, postmodernism and postcolonialism with an acknowledgement of the androcentric and Eurocentric holds of power on anthropology and ethnography. Foucault's discourse on the knowledge of power is critical to understanding the difference between knowledge produced by Western feminist writers and feminist ethnographers of the Global South (5). 'Thus, issues of representation, positionalities, location, and the production and reproduction of social identities surface as the crucial questions for feminist ethnographers today' (3). The works of Lila Abu-Lughod, Judith Stacey, Kamala Visweswaran and Radhika Parameswaran are important for understanding the feminist ethnography of the present age (3). Kamala Visweswaran writes that the method of feminist ethnography will challenge the traditional tendency of citing epics written by men and considering the works of female ethnographers as 'subjective' at the same time (1994, 17). She also says, 'A feminist ethnography could focus on women's relationship to other women and the power differentials between them' (20). During the second wave of feminism, feminists were positioned in a contradictory place due to their opposition to biological essentialism or universalism, and they promoted cultural relativism as a mode of organising universal sisterhood (18). Visweswaran also elaborates that women and feminist workers of Third World countries had objections to American feminists generalising women's issues, and they accused the traditional mode of feminism of being racist and homogenised. Anthropologists resolved the issue with their approach to cultural relativism for the sake of a heterogenised and context-specific lens to evaluate women's issues (20).

Ethnographic works by anthropologists need to be evaluated as well to maintain objectivity because, nowadays, human subject research is not free from fabrication and the politics of representation. Laurel

Richardson of Ohio State University, Columbus, suggests in his article that 'ethnography needs to be evaluated through two lenses: science and arts' (2000, 253). As ethnographers want to frame their works as 'scientific' as well as 'literary', they endeavour to remove the gaps between 'fact' and 'fiction', 'subjective' and 'objective', and 'true' and 'imagined' (253). So, the result of an ethnographic work can belong to several genres like 'creative nonfiction; fiction; ethnographic fiction; the nonfiction novel; and true fiction' (253). Richardson argues that postmodernism brought liberal ideas to ethnographic studies by freeing the ethnographers to represent their studies in different ways. At the same time, it narrows the authors' approach by asking them to be conscious of authorship, truth and validity of ideas (253–254). When someone wants to evaluate an ethnographic work, Richardson suggests, 'It is our continuing task to create new criteria and new criteria for choosing criteria' (2000, 254). In this article, he provides us with five matrixes for evaluating an ethnographic work: substantive contribution, aesthetic merit, reflexivity, impact and express reality. Feminist ethnography shares a broad connection to the ethnographic research methodology. Hence, select matrixes defined by Richardson have been utilised in this book to evaluate feminist ethnographic texts of the 1971 war.

Women of the 1971 War in Feminist Narratives

Unlike Western feminism, Third World feminism and women's issues in the context of those nations have received very little attention (Mohanty 2003, 45). Writings of South Asia, which are also much influenced by the writings of the West, have shown women's agency very rarely. Hence, women's experiences in the war and their roles in nation-building in South Asia is much ignored. Due to a popular generalisation of South Asian women as raped and victimised in war narratives, the subject of the women of the war in Bangladesh remained untouched to an extent by academicians in their discussion of nationalism and nation-building (D'Costa 2011, 9). Recent feminist narratives (in the form of fiction and non-fiction) on the 1971 war have tried to relocate women's traditional role in the war history and talk about women's agency in nation-building. Fictional narratives have been vital sources to trace the truths of genocide and war crimes over the decades. The 1971 war has received special attention in the literature of South Asian regions and their diasporas for the last three decades. Apart from Bangladeshi writings, the war is one of the important political settings in Salman Rushdie's *Midnight's Children* ([1981] 2013), Amitav Ghosh's *The Shadow Lines* (2011), Kamila Shamsie's *Kartography* (2002), Sorayya Khan's *Noor* (2004) and so on. Since 1971, Bangladeshi literary and visual representation are preoccupied with the glory of the Liberation War, the deeds of freedom fighters and the heroic tales of the Birangona. Bangladeshi writing in English also emerges as a genre in which Bangladesh's freedom struggle and the issues of gender have been much prioritised. A feminist intervention is essential because war is portrayed in history as a men's game. While history fails to acknowledge the contribution of women in the freedom struggle of Bangladesh, Bangladeshi diasporic writers such as Tahmima Anam and Dilruba Z. Ara use instances from their real-life experiences of women to glorify their deeds in fictional narratives. Anam's parents campaigned for the war in 1971, and the plot of Anam's book *A Golden Age* (2007) is much inspired by her grandmother's story of their house being raided by the Pakistani army (Armitstead 2016). Anam's novel tells the story of widowed Rehana Haque, whose struggle for identity and the custody of her children during the 1971 war resembles the struggle of Bangladesh. Her courage in helping freedom fighters by sheltering them and hiding their weapons, while inspiring her son and daughter to work for the country, exemplifies the role of women in the war. Ara's novel *Blame* (2015) is a stunning tale of the 'unsung heroines' of the 1971 war as mentioned by the author in an interview with the *Dhaka Tribune* (Haque 2016). Through the characters of Laila and Geeta, Ara shows how women took up arms and participated in the freedom struggle and became victims in the same war. Ara also shows in this novel that the blame game is a part of the war game, and women are the worst victims. As the 1971 war was an ethnic struggle between Bangladesh and Pakistan, the war influenced the lives of Urdu-speaking people in Bangladesh as well as the Bengali-speaking people of Pakistan. Pakistani writers such as Kamila Shamsie and Sorayya Khan wrote about the fate of Bengali-speaking women in Pakistan in the context of the ethnic conflict in 1971. Kamila Shamsie's novel *Kartography* shows how ethnic hatred crosses the boundary and touches the lives of women like Maheen, a Bengali woman living in Karachi (2002). In Shamsie's novel, Maheen's marginalisation in Karachi exemplifies how women share solidarity based on their ethnicity and form their cartography of struggle across political or geographical barriers. Such narratives of women of the 1971 war in fiction reconstruct history through an assertion that women had significant roles in the war and deserve recognition in the historiography.

For decades, writers and activists have focused on non-fictional narratives to portray the lives of people against the backdrop of the 1971 war. Non-fictional war narratives about the lives of women also exist, such as the autobiography of Bangladeshi writer and activist Jahanara Imam (1929–1994)—*Ekattorer Dinguli* (The days of 71; 1986). On 25 March 1971, war erupted in the whole country, and many youngsters like Jahanara Imam's son Shafi Imam Rumi participated in the war as freedom fighters. Jahanara Imam records those days of uncertainty and anxiety and her feelings as a mother of a freedom fighter in her account. Imam, who was popularly known as *Shaheed Janani* (martyr's mother), later played an important role in setting up the *Gono Adalat* (the public tribunal) in 1992 for a mass movement against the killers and collaborators of the 1971 war (Sun 2019). Basanti Guhathakurta's *Ekattorer Smriti* (Memory of 71), which was published in 1991, is another non-fictional narrative that is the author's personal account. She was the wife of Bengali intellectual and University of Dhaka lecturer Jyotirmoy Guhathakurta, who was brutally shot before his family members and died a few days later. Guhathakurta, in her memoir, gives the account of her survival with her daughter Meghna during the nine months of the freedom struggle, and her struggle is linked with the nation's struggle. The non-fictional narrative that has remained most discussed and cited over time is Neelima Ibrahim's *Aami Birangona Balchi* (1994). Ibrahim's book is probably the first specimen of narrative non-fiction to document the lives of real rape victims of the 1971 war. The genre of documenting the oral history of the 1971 war started with the publication of Ibrahim's book, which contains the narratives of seven Birangona. Ibrahim's book later gave rise to a few more narratives that documented the voices of the women who were associated with the war. Another book that documents the lives of real Birangona vividly and minutely is Nayanika Mookherjee's book *The Spectral Wound: Sexual Violence, Public Memories, and the Bangladesh War of 1971* (2015b). Mookherjee records the stories of four Birangona from Enayetpur, a village in western Bangladesh. Alongside them, she also documents the stories of seven more Birangona from the rest of the country (Mookherjee 2015b, 5). Her ethnographic work in Bangladesh was initiated to chronicle the real stories from the post-war trajectories of Birangona, defying the politics of representation in history and popular culture. We have also looked at other non-fictional accounts of the survival stories of non-Bengali women in connection with the 1971 war. Sarmila Bose's book *Dead Reckoning: Memories of the 1971 Bangladesh War* (2011a) and Yasmin Saikia's book *Women, War and the Making of Bangladesh: Remembering 1971* (2011b) are examples of oral history that report the lives of rape survivors in Bangladesh in vivid details with a special focus on Bihari women's victimisation by Bengali nationalists and Bengali women's victimisation by their native people. Though women's accounts in narrative non-fiction are often accused of being fabricated, biased and exaggerated, these narratives play significant roles in portraying the plight of women during the war and in its aftermath beyond their representation in seemingly gendered historiography.

After an extended literature review, the authors of this book infer that women's multidimensional experiences in the context of the 1971 war, as covered in ethnographic literature, are fragmented and have not been consolidated in a singular work. There have been a few historiographies as well as ethnographic works on the war, but there is hardly any book that evaluates existing ethnographic narratives on the same war through a feminist lens. This book analyses the discriminatory and gendered nature of the history of the 1971 war and also evaluates the representation of women in feminist ethnographic literature (both fiction and non-fiction) to focus on women's agency, survival and post-war trajectories. Finally, this book endeavours to show how the feminist ethnographic narratives of the war challenge the politics of representing women in traditional historiography.

Brief Outline of the Chapters

In the five chapters of this book, 'Introduction: The Gendered History of the 1971 War and Women's Narratives' (the first chapter) is a brief outline that sets the context. This introduction traverses world history, particularly the history of the 1971 war in Bangladesh, to substantiate the claims that women's position in the archives is negligible. As history seems to be gendered in interpreting women's association with the 1971 war, this book resorts to feminist ethnographic narratives (both fictional and non-fictional) to trace and curate women's position in the war. The politics of representation involved in representing women in war narratives has been discussed with theoretical references from the writings of Stuart J. Hall (1997) and Gayatri Chakravorty Spivak (1988). The feminist ethnographic narratives are evaluated briefly through Richardson's model (2000). An extensive literature review has been done in this section to identify the gap area. The literature review also suggests more references to women's engagement and their survival in the war. Finally, the chapter ends with a brief outline of the chapters ahead and future scope.

The second chapter, 'Relocating the Women of the 1971 War in History', is a feminist reading of select historiography of the 1971 war. As the Liberation War engaged Bangladesh, Pakistan and India almost directly, at least one representative historical account has been chosen from each nation. First, the history of Bangladesh is evaluated through the feminist lens of Cook (2006), Saikia (2011b), Mookherjee (2015b) and D'Costa (2011). The two books that have been read for this purpose are Zafar Iqbal's *Muktijuddher Itihas* (2008) and the Bangladesh government's official publication *Bangladesher Shadhinota Juddha: Dolilpotro* ([1982] 2009). Zafar Iqbal has written a very short but compact history of Bangladesh's political journey in his account. Though he has mentioned that women contributed a lot to the freedom struggle of Bangladesh, their contribution is not elaborated as a historical or chronological study. The official document of Bangladesh, which is a detailed account of the Bangladesh Liberation War comprising almost 12,000 pages and is divided into fifteen volumes, mentions women in a few random pages as victims of rape and violence (Rahman [1982] 2009, 554). The next book, *1971: A Global History of the Creation of Bangladesh*, is by Srinath Raghavan, a noted Indian historian who broadly discusses the foreign issues related to the 1971 war, Indira Gandhi's role in freeing Bangladesh and the diplomacy of India and Pakistan behind the war and the creation of Bangladesh (2013). Surprisingly, even Raghavan has not touched upon the issue of rape and gendered violence perpetrated on women. Not only that, he also avoids commenting on women's agency in this war. Iftikhar Malik's *The History of Pakistan* has been discussed here to look into the history of the 1971 war from Pakistan's perspective (2008). Malik has overlooked the controversy over the number of deaths and the intensity of gendered violence in the 1971 war. The history of the war has been read from a global perspective in Willem van

Schendel's book *A History of Bangladesh* (2009). Unlike the previous account, Schendel's book acknowledges women's agency in the 1971 war by referring to literary narratives of Bangladeshi writers such as Sufia Kamal (165). The conclusion of the second chapter discusses the gendered nature of historical narratives with a resolution that fictional and non-fictional narratives of women writers and ethnographers such as Dilruba Z. Ara, Tahmima Anam, Kamila Shamsie, Neelima Ibrahim, Nayanika Mookherjee, Yasmin Saikia and Sarmila Bose can be vital weapons to trace women's position in the history of the 1971 war.

The third chapter, 'Women of the 1971 War in Fictional Narratives', points out the necessity of women's narratives to reframe the gendered history of the 1971 war. Notable feminist Margaret Homans discusses why studies in narratives are seminal in interdisciplinary studies and research. She refers to an anthropologist who represents a culture and celebrates storytelling through writing a novel titled *Their Eyes* (1994, 8). Citing feminist critics such as Kamala Visweswaran and Sanjukta Ghosh, the third chapter elaborates on the connection between ethnographic interventions and the feminist novels of the 1971 war like Dilruba Z. Ara's *Blame* (2015) and Tahmima Anam's *A Golden Age* (2007). Based on Ara's own experiences with the victims and activists of the 1971 war, her novel showcases the lives of two war rape survivors Laila and Gita, who become ostracised and the agents of blame in post-war Bangladesh after fighting bravely in the war. Tahmima Anam utilises her professional experience of being an anthropologist to portray the life of Rehana, a courageous lady who sacrifices her son and daughter and helps other freedom fighters to liberate Bangladesh. Postcolonial feminist Chandra Talpade Mohanty implies that the traditional definition and the context of feminism, our endeavour to foreground certain contexts over others and the continuous shifts of the conceptual cartographies are all crucial in the formation of the cartographies of the Third World women (2003, 45). The third section of this chapter elaborates on the formation of such cartographies of the struggle of migrant Bengali women in Karachi against the backdrop of the ethnic hatred in/after the 1971 war as shown in Kamila Shamsie's novel *Kartography* (2002). With a close reading of these three texts as feminist ethnographic texts followed by evaluation through Richardson's ethnographic model, this chapter talks about how fictional narratives of the 1971 war have endeavoured to route their roots of women's engagement in the war and their plight in postcolonial society.

The fourth chapter, 'Women of the 1971 War in Narrative Non-fiction', begins with a discussion on the emergence of narrative non-fiction to investigate the truth about genocide in the 20th and 21st centuries. Based on the theoretical frameworks of feminist ethnographers such as Sanjukta Ghosh, Kristin Aune and Kamala Visweswaran, this chapter also points out the necessity of feminist ethnography for a culturally relative and contextual study of the lives of women who were engaged in the 1971 war. Using Chakraborty Spivak's theory that the subaltern can speak if they can bypass the politics of representation (1988, 25), this chapter elaborates a few feminist ethnographers' endeavours to make the subaltern voice public, defying the patriarchal representation of women in the history of the 1971 war. The Birangona and their role in making Bangladesh are described with references to the feminist ethnographic literature of Neelima Ibrahim's *A War Heroine, I Speak* (2017, translated from the 1994 Bengali text *Aami Birangona Balchi*) and Nayanika Mookherjee's *The Spectral Wound: Sexual Violence, Public Memories and the Bangladesh war of 1971* (2015b). The following section covers the victimisation of non-Bengali people, focusing on non-Bengali women, by Bengali nationalists after the 1971 war, with illustrations from the narratives in Sarmila Bose's *Dead Reckoning: Memories of the 1971 Bangladesh War* (2011a) and Yasmin Saikia's *Women, War, and the Making of Bangladesh: Remembering 1971* (2011b). This chapter also evaluates women's location in the unknown register of the archive of the 1971 war through the references in Saikia's book, which presents the narratives of the real survivors of the wars: the women who tell their stories as 'agents of change, as social workers, caregivers, and wartime fighters' (Saikia 2011b, Synopsis). The chapter ends by validating the claims made by the authors with sources like interviews, newspaper articles and counter-narratives. It also evaluates these four texts as feminist ethnographic texts followed by the evaluation of ethnography through Richardson's model (2000).

The last chapter, 'Feminist Narratives of 1971: the Present and the Future' (Chapter 5), discusses the politics of representation of women in the historical accounts of Bangladesh. It also reflects upon how the emergence of contemporary feminist ethnographic narratives has vehemently restructured seemingly gendered history with a transition of facts into tales or narratives in which women find their position in the centre instead of as sporadic mentions. Following the trends of feminist ethnography and postcolonial feminism, the concluding chapter locates women's position in the 1971 war and their postcolonial plights as context-specific rather than generalising them. Finally, the ending of this chapter opens up the scope of research for future researchers in the areas of humanities, anthropology, cultural studies and gender studies.

Conclusion

Bangladesh celebrated the fiftieth anniversary of its independence in 2021, but the historical accounts of women's victimhood and agency in the 1971 war are still conflicting. Our book follows a postmodern feminist methodology to evaluate women's narratives of the 1971 war from the literary representations of contemporary ethnographers and writers. We do not want to settle the truth connected to gender violence and women's roles in the war. Instead, we wish to reach closer to it through the representation of multidimensional and conflicting narratives and their systematic evaluation. The methodology and findings of this book may widen the scope for future researchers who want to go for interdisciplinary research on ethnic conflicts, gender violence, women's victimhood and agency in the context of South Asia.

Notes

1 'Birangona' was a title conferred upon the women who survived sexual violence in the 1971 war after the independence of Bangladesh by the then President Sheikh Mujibur Rahman to honour their sacrifice for the nation and to rehabilitate them.

2 The image was widely circulated during the Liberation War with a tagline *Banglar Mayera Meyera Sobai Muktijoddha* [All the women of Bangladesh are freedom fighters]. See Mitra (2012).

3 Neelima Ibrahim was a feminist activist and a pioneer in the rape survivors' rehabilitation process during and after the Liberation War of Bangladesh. She was also a professor of the University of Dhaka, Bangladesh, and authored the book *Aami Birangona Balchi*.

4 The book was published in Bengali in 1994. Then it was translated into English by Fayeza Hasanat of the University of Central Florida, United States of America, and published as *A War Heroine, I Speak* in 2017. This research refers to the translated version of the book.

5 Muhammad Ali Jinnah (1876–1948) proposed the two-nation theory that resulted in the creation of Pakistan in 1947 on the basis of religious identity of the majority. He served as Pakistan's first governor-general.

6 The Language Movement in 1952 was initiated by the students and youngsters of East Pakistan to protest against the Pakistani government's decision to impose Urdu as the only national language of East Pakistan where most of the people's mother tongue was Bengali. On 21 February 1952, many student revolutionists of the University of Dhaka were shot dead by the then Pakistani police. In 1999, UNESCO declared 21 February as the International Mother Language Day to commemorate their sacrifice for their mother tongue.

7 Bengali refers to the major ethnic group of Bangladesh and the Indian states of West Bengal and Tripura whose mother tongue is Bengali.

8 Sheikh Mujibur Rahman (1920–1975) was the founding President of the Republic of Bangladesh. During the freedom struggle, he was a very popular leader who declared the independence of Bangladesh on 26 March 1971. He is popularly known as *Bangabandhu* or the friend of Bengal. On 15 August 1975, he, along with his other family members, were assassinated by enemies. Only his two daughters survived because they were abroad at the time.

9 Yahya Khan (1917–1980) was a Pakistani general and also the third President of Pakistan. As per Bangladeshi historical narratives, the 1971 genocide happened under his active leadership.

10 Zulfikar Ali Bhutto (1928–1979) was the ninth Prime Minister of Pakistan.

11 Muktibahini refers to the Bangladeshi freedom fighters who collaborated with the Indian Army to liberate their nation from Pakistan.

12 Indira Gandhi (1917–1984) was an Indian National Congress leader and the first female Prime Minister of India.

13 Razakars refer to those Bengali people who collaborated with the Pakistani military in the 1971 war to initiate genocide and gender violence.

14 Third World countries refer to mainly those of Asia and Africa that belong to an economically inferior position in global index; see Banton (2020).

15 Bihari refers to an ethnic group of India, mainly from the state of Bihar.

16 Ziaur Rahman or Major Ziaur Rahman (1936–1981) was a Bangladeshi army officer turned politician. He served as the President of Bangladesh from 1977 to 1981.

17 Hussain Muhammad Ershad (1930–2019) was a Bangladeshi army Chief turned politician who served as the president of Bangladesh from 1983 to 1990.

2

Relocating the Women of the 1971 War in History

> One of the greatest shortcomings in the perception of our fight for Independence is our consistent failure to recognise the role of women in our Liberation War. In fact, the role of women is largely ignored, denied and misconstrued in our mainstream history. This is because of our general tendency to think of war only in terms of physical fighting and exchange of gunshots.
>
> —A.M. Amin, L.A. Ahmed and S. Ahsan, 'The Women in Our Liberation War'

Introduction

Since the advent of civilisation, history has remained the domain of men, and women have mostly been represented as passive, subjugated and tradition-bound. Texts or narratives based on historical events have generally reserved their applause for men, incessantly valorising their contribution. In this context, these texts have often generated criticism, especially from feminists who consider them to be biased towards men and believe that they sideline the contributions made by women. This reliance on fixed history in the postmodern age, when post-structuralism is the dominating theoretical concern of gender and cultural studies, is very contradictory. The fixity of knowledge, whether scientific or ideological, was already questioned by post-structuralist thinkers such as Roland Barthes and Jacques Derrida in the 1960s. Interdisciplinary studies in humanities in the 21st century also advocate the relativity of knowledge, and hence, more and more narratives attempt to refigure historical representations. So, contemporary academia has endeavoured to answer the most critical question in the studies of historiography in the present age: 'Can there be a post-structural history?' (Bolla et al. 1986, 49).

The history of the 1971 war remains fragmented, contested and misrepresented, even though the nation celebrated the golden jubilee year of its independence in 2021. The main reason is the lack of proper evidence and investigation into the history of the 1971 war through an academic lens. While the Rwandan Genocide and the American Holocaust have been able to create a strong appeal among academicians to work on them, the war of 1971 in Bangladesh has slipped out of public awareness despite a probable loss of over three million lives (Boissoneault 2016). When the International Crimes Tribunal (United Nations Court) was established in 1993 to seek international justice for genocide and rape worldwide, surprisingly, the genocide and gendered violence in Bangladesh got hardly any mention (Linton 2010a, 187). Three South Asian nations—Bangladesh, Pakistan and India—were directly involved in the war. A few nations like America and Soviet Russia were external motivators behind the war. The historiography of Bangladesh, India and Pakistan mostly deals with the internal ethnic politics between the Bengali-speaking people of Bangladesh (then East Pakistan) and the Urdu-speaking people of undivided Pakistan, whereas a few international historians such as Gary J. Bass and Srinath Raghavan talk about the external politics of America and Soviet Russia behind the war. Gary J. Bass's *The Blood Telegram* (2012) takes its title from the historical telegram of the then American consul general Archer Blood, who wrote to Dhaka declaring his and his staff's opposition to the US government's stance on the freedom struggle of East Pakistan (Purushothaman 2012, 461). Bass's book also deals with America's diplomatic policy to patronise Pakistan with arms and all types of support so that it could make Pakistan a link to its ally China. At the same time, the book shows India and Soviet Russia's endeavour to free Bangladesh from Pakistan to destroy that motive of America.

However, this kind of external politics hardly came into focus in the post-1971 historiographies of Bangladesh, India and Pakistan. The present historical accounts of the Liberation War of Bangladesh mainly focus on ethnic discrimination, Pakistani leaders' hunger for power, their ignorance, the injustices perpetrated and the struggle of the Bengali ethnic community at the hands of the Pakistani military during the nine months of the freedom struggle. These accounts, including Bangladeshi ones, dealing with the Liberation War are vague. The lack of scientific research, systematic documentation and academic intervention is apparent. Empirical evidence about how many people died, how many women were raped and how many war babies were adopted by foreign nationals is missing (Hossain 2006). One more factor is the intervention of the Bangladeshi government: each time the government changes and a new government comes into power, history is modified as per their ideology by destroying the previous documents on the 1971 war (Mohaiemen 2012).

Tragically, the historians and the policy makers of Bangladesh have neglected the women's roles and agencies in the 1971 war of Bangladesh to date. Bangladesh, as a free nation, celebrated the golden jubilee of its independence in 2021, but its history is still politicised and gendered. Most texts, historical or otherwise, restrict themselves to the period from the 1947 Partition to the 1971 war and the birth of Bangladesh. The domestic and social struggles, especially of women, have been completely overlooked or extensively bypassed (Saikia 2004, 275). In the case of the historiography of the Liberation War of Bangladesh, women are only mentioned as rape victims and treated as statistics. The stories of their courage, active participation and power of resistance have been either avoided or conveniently suppressed. The greatest shortcoming of the history of Bangladesh is its failure to recognise the women who once fought in the war as guerrilla fighters, served as nurses to the wounded soldiers and sacrificed their lives and chastity for Bangladesh (Amin et al. 2016). Neither the official documents nor the other historical accounts mention their contribution because war has always been thought of as a men's game. This chapter discusses five historical texts to trace history's dealings with the women who faced the 1971 war. The five books discussed here are Muhammad Zafar Iqbal's *Muktijuddher Itihas* (2008), the Bangladesh government's official publication *Bangladesher Shadhinota Juddha: Dolilpotro* (first published in 1982, reprinted in 2009), Srinath Raghavan's *1971: A Global History of the Creation of Bangladesh* (2013), Iftikhar Malik's *The History of Pakistan* (2008) and Willem van Schendel's *A History of Bangladesh* (2009). After discussing women's position in history, this chapter examines why feminist intervention is needed to bring women's narratives of bravery and survival in/after the war into existence. The present book aims to reread the historical representation of women in the historiographies of the Bangladesh Liberation War to establish the imperatives of reframing history focusing on the feministic paradigm.

What Does the History Say?

The 1971 Liberation War of Bangladesh, an ethnic-cum-political conflict, directly engaged three nations: Bangladesh, Pakistan and India. Muhammad Zafar Iqbal, a Bangladeshi historian and novelist, presents a very compact and informative history of Bangladesh in his book *Muktijuddher Itihas* (2008). The book traces the roots of Bangladesh's freedom struggle, starting from the Lahore Resolution of 1940 and the Partition of 1947, followed by the creation of two separate nations based on religion, Hindu-majority India and Muslim-majority Pakistan. The author criticises the notion of creating a nation based only on religion despite the ethnic diversity. Pakistan became a nation of unique demographical variations with its two parts scattered to the two sides of a completely different independent country, India, at a distance of approximately two thousand kilometres. The geographical dislocation and ethnic and language diversity could hardly unite Pakistan based on a single religion (Iqbal 2008, 1–2). The genocide started in Bangladesh on 25 March 1971 with Operation Searchlight. The Bengali community, especially intellectuals and Hindus, were targeted, and 5,000 to 10,000 Bengalis were killed in a single night (Townsend 2017). Iqbal's historical account gives a vivid description of Operation Searchlight and the ensuing suffering and trauma of the people of Bangladesh. Led by Yahya Khan, the Pakistani military launched genocide in Dhaka on 25 March, killing civilians, soldiers, students of the University of Dhaka and intellectuals of the country. To keep the event unrecorded, international journalists were forced to leave the country before this incident, though a journalist named Simon Dring reported the horrific developments in Dhaka in the *Washington Post* on the next day (Iqbal 2008, 7). Operation Searchlight ended with the arrest of Sheikh Mujibur Rahman who declared the independence of Bangladesh on 26 March 1971 before being arrested (8). Thereafter, the genocide spread throughout the country, targeting civilians and, particularly, the Hindu community (10). Students, peasants and civilians from the plains and the hills joined the war with minimum arms and no professional training (12). Zafar Iqbal acknowledges that the history of Bangladesh's freedom struggle remains incomplete if the contribution of the women is not mentioned. Women encouraged their male counterparts, helped them to carry on with their mission and, at times, engaged in armed combat (13, 18). Unlike other historians, Iqbal has acknowledged the other side of the cruelty of the 1971 war—the killing and abduction of Bihari men and women by Bengali nationalists in the aftermath (18). Iqbal's book also acknowledges the stateless condition of the Bihari community in the Geneva Camp[1] of Bangladesh even after five decades of Bangladeshi independence. The Pakistani government refused to rehabilitate the community in Pakistan (18). Iqbal discusses the controversy about the number of martyrs and raped women. He claims that two hundred and fifty thousand women were raped by the Pakistani army and the Razakar militia, and the death toll, as speculated in Bangladesh, is over three million (18–19).

The next book and one of the most important documents on the Liberation War to be reread through the feminist lens is *Bangladesher Shadhinota Juddha: Dolilpotro* (The Liberation War of Bangladesh: A Deed; [1982] 2009), the official record of the timeline of the war archived by the Government of Bangladesh. The Government of Bangladesh intended to preserve the history of the war and, hence, formed a committee named Jatiya Swadhinotar Itihas Parishad between 1972 and 1973 to document the same. The outcome of this project was the *Dolilpotro* (literally historical deed), edited by Hasan Hafizur Rahman and other historians like Afsan Chowdhury and Dr Sukumar Biswas (Hossain 2006). It is a voluminous chronological record spanning fifteen volumes and containing almost 12,000 pages. The first two volumes narrate the context of the war after the 1947 Partition. The next four volumes of the book describe the formation of the Mujibnagar government[2] and its preparation to monitor the war. The seventh volume deals with the official announcements and deeds by the West Pakistani government regarding their demand for and support of a united Pakistan. The eighth volume discusses the genocide, the mass rape and the refugee crisis that followed the massacre on the night of 25 March 1971. The nine-month freedom struggle between the allied forces of Bangladesh and India and the Pakistani military is covered in the next three volumes of the book. The twelfth volume discusses India's contribution to the freedom movement and its recognition of Bangladesh as a free country. The thirteenth volume discusses the recognition of Bangladesh as an independent country by the United Nations Organization (UNO) and the reactions of other nations to Bangladesh's independence. The fourteenth volume discusses the world's opinion about independent Bangladesh and the initiatives of international organisations to rehabilitate the war victims. The fifteenth volume documents the interviews of noted politicians and activists who were directly associated with the war. Though this is an elaborate official historiography of the 1971 war, it fails to represent gender issues with due importance.

This historical deed of Bangladesh presents not only the context of the political upheaval in the 1960s and 1970s in East Pakistan but also the representation of the 1971 war in international media to justify the claim that the Pakistani army played a crucial role in the brutalities, mass rape and genocide. In Volume VII, the book takes up a series of articles that appeared in international media about the violence perpetrated in East Pakistan. One such article by Anthony Lewis, published in the *New York Times* on 7 June 1971, claims that the principal agent of death and violence was the Pakistani army, whose killings were very selective. Their targets were intellectuals, leaders, doctors, teachers and educationists (Rahman [1982] 2009, 554). One report in the *New York Times*, published on 4 July 1971, highlights the communal image of the war. The report claims that anti-Pakistan Muslims were killed by the Pakistani army, but Hindus were the special targets. Muslims were encouraged by the Pakistani army to loot Hindu houses, burn them and perpetrate all types of violence upon them (555). These reports highlight the political and communal issues related to the 1971 war, but the gender issues remain untouched. References to women being tortured, raped and marginalised only appear in a few places: 'Men, women, and children were bayonetted to death. Women were raped. About 200,000 people were reported to have been killed. Millions of people began their escape into India' (554).

Volume XI of *Dolilpotro* has a transcript of a radio talk by Colonel M.A.G. Osmani, the commander-in-chief of the Muktibahini. In this radio talk, Osmani spoke of different stories of valiant acts of the Muktibahini. He portrayed in detail the genocide perpetrated by Yahya Khan that led the West Pakistani force to wreak havoc in the first six months of the war. Osmani suggests in his speech that the act of killing intellectual people, educationists, students, soldiers and civilians was done to ensure the destruction of the backbone of the ethnic Bengali community. He praised the actions of the Muktibahini who had endeavoured to free different areas from the control of Pakistani rule and offered prize money for their valiant acts. In a few places, Osmani did mention girls and women in his speech, but he did not refer to women's participation in the freedom struggle. On the other hand, he repeatedly called the Muktibahini 'brave sons'. In his long speech, he stated:

> The orgy began. That night in the city at Dacca alone many thousands of men, women and children were killed. The genocide, in fact undeclared aggression, unleashed that night followed a preplanned pattern when millions including educationists, philosophers, scientists, doctors, promising youth (our hopes for tomorrow) laborers, poor bread earners, children in mother's arms, unarmed Bengali Officers and Men of the regular forces were brutally done to death. Women including minor girls were raped and killed and many were forced to walk naked. (Rahman [1982] 2009, 184–188)

Volume XI of *Dolilpotro* documents the press releases of the Bangladesh Forces. Through these press releases, the Muktibahini spread the news of atrocities performed by the Pakistani forces in different places. A few common attributes of the press releases are reports of the atrocities of the Pakistani force, the bravery of the Muktibahini and the imprisonment of women and their transformation into victims. There are many tales of the men's valour, but women could hardly get rid of the tag of being prisoners and victims of the Pakistani troops. One such press release of the Muktibahini on 23 November 1971 from Mujibnagar says:

> Bhurungamari along with a large tract of northern Rangpur was liberated by Mukti Bahini on the night 14/15th of November.... Every one of 500 people who were held captive had similar miserable tales to tell. While the women were imprisoned in the office building they were not allowed even to go out to answer their natural calls when they wanted. (Rahman [1982] 2009, 192–193)

The authenticity of the historical accounts of the 1971 war by the South Asian historians has been questioned on various occasions not only by international academicians but also by Bangladeshi scholars and media writers. The accuracy of facts regarding gender issues is sometimes dubious. The *Daily Star*, one of the leading national English newspapers in Bangladesh, published an article titled 'The Women in our Liberation War: Tales of Endurance and Courage' on the occasion of Victory Day[3] in 2016 to reclaim the role of women in the formation of the nation. Aasha Mehreen Amin, Lavina Ambreen Ahmed and Shamim Ahsan, the writers of the article, claim that the historiography of independent Bangladesh has continuously failed to recognise women as contributors to the freedom movement because war is always considered physical fighting with guns and bombs. The narratives of the bravery of male freedom fighters dominate the Bangladeshi psyche because of the improper representation of women, who are only described as victimised, oppressed and left to suffer by the tormentors. History fails to acknowledge the other sides of war where women sheltered the freedom fighters, motivated their sons and relatives to join the war, nursed wounded freedom fighters during the war and had the courage to survive after being raped and tortured by the enemy (Amin et al. 2016).

History, intentionally, unintentionally or politically, sidelined the role and contribution of women in the making of Bangladesh. This biased approach does not only apply to the historical narratives by Bangladeshi historians but also to those by the other South Asian historians. Srinath Raghavan's recently published historical anthology on the 1971 war, titled *1971: A Global History of the Creation of Bangladesh* (2013), also makes no special place for women freedom fighters and victims. The book does not mention the rape victims, their transformation into Birangona, their survival with their war babies and their marginalisation in Bangladesh after independence. While the book comprehensively encapsulates Bangladesh's political journey to achieve independence from Pakistan, Raghavan mysteriously refrains from writing about women in the freedom struggle. The book is widely acclaimed by international academicians for fuelling historical debate by insisting on the role of former Indian prime minister Indira Gandhi (1917–1984) in the separation of Bangladesh from Pakistan. However, it remains surprisingly silent on the brutality of mass rape and gendered violence that took place in East Pakistan (Carter 2014, 520–521). The author has chosen to take a neutral side in the controversy regarding the exact number of martyrs and victims. He suggests that the 'figure is speculative' (Raghavan 2013, 12). Despite being titled *1971: A Global History of the Creation of Bangladesh*, the book has not touched upon the history of brutality behind the creation of Bangladesh. Raghavan focuses on the international agendas behind the creation of Bangladesh, from Washington DC to Moscow, Delhi and Dhaka. He emphasises one thing: the creation of Bangladesh was inevitable due to the geographical distance between East Pakistan and West Pakistan and due to the long-resented discrimination faced by the people of East Pakistan (Ganguly 2016, 194). The elaboration on external foreign policy and the suppression of internal chaos, genocide and rape in Raghavan's book aligns his writing with Gary J. Bass's book *The Blood Telegram: Nixon, Kissinger and a Forgotten Genocide* (2013). In addition to internal ethnic issues, both the books endeavour to explore the politics of nations such as India and the United States of America behind the 1971 war. Both the books detail India's motives for separation and America's purposes in keeping Pakistan undivided at any cost. David Carter says, '[Both] books are a telling reminder of the risks from highly personalised national leadership, insufficiently checked by robust institutions, and of its long-term adverse consequences' (2014, 520). The gendered perspective of the Liberation War of Bangladesh, like women's participation in the movement, Bengali women's victimisation during the war, Bihari women's victimisation after the war and women's role in the peace process, are completely absent in Raghavan's historiography. Though Raghavan has mentioned a few feminist writings such as those of Nayanika Mookherjee and Yasmin

Saikia in the reference section, their portrayal of women's narratives has not found any place in the main text of his historiography.

Iftikhar Malik's *The History of Pakistan* (2008) is a landmark historical book to read the history of the 1971 war from Pakistan's perspective. Malik's historiography acknowledges the growing dissatisfaction of the people of East Pakistan after the Partition till 1971 due to the centralisation of power and unequal distribution of resources. East Pakistanis felt that Pakistan always prioritised its west wing over the east wing (Malik 2008, 153–154). The book also discusses the general election of 1970 in East Pakistan under the supervision of Ayub Khan[4] (1907–1974). The Awami League, led by Mujib, gained a massive victory due to the support of the East Pakistani people. The people resented the West Pakistani ruler for the indifference of the Pakistani central government during floods and the devastating cyclone in Bhola (a coastal town in East Pakistan) in 1970. When the resentment gained momentum amongst the people of East Pakistan because elected leaders were denied the chance to form a government, Yahya Khan and his close associate Zulfikar Ali Bhutto flew to East Pakistan to control the violence. Their initiative (known as Operation Searchlight) turned into a genocide with the intervention of Pakistani military forces (Malik 2008, 155). Most of these events have been placed in the political timeline of Malik's book, but surprisingly, the writer has avoided talking about the number of deaths and rape victims in the nine-month-long freedom struggle in Bangladesh. When international historiographers such as Willem van Schendel (2009) and Bina D'Costa (2011) have substantiated the gendered violence in the 1971 war and women's courageous role in the same war, the silence of modern Pakistani historians such as Iftikhar Malik and others over the matter only indicates that Pakistan intends to forget the bitter memory of genocide and rape through its exclusion from the nation's history.

Over the decades, global historians have contributed a lot to the investigation of the myths and facts surrounding the 1971 war. Five decades after the independence of Bangladesh, research on the war is still primarily dependent on the references and claims made by global historians because Bangladesh, India and Pakistan have failed to produce sufficient scholarly works on the subject. Though many recent narratives claim that the number of victims of the genocide is exaggerated to an extent by the Bangladesh government, portrayals by global historians shows that Pakistan's tendency to hide the intensity of the brutality cannot be denied. While discussing the role of Bangladeshi women in the war, Willem van Schendel's book *A History of Bangladesh* provides a substantial account of gender issues (2009). The twenty-two chapters of the book give a comprehensive history of Bangladesh starting from the Mughal period up to the present time. The last seven chapters of the book present the post-war society of Bangladesh, Bangladesh's rise as one of the economically strong countries in South Asia, and Bangladeshi women's empowerment and power of resistance. Schendel is very critical of the identity crisis faced by Bangladeshi people nowadays. The rich tradition of Bengali culture and the Bengali people's humanistic approach, non-secularism, and association with the heritage of Rabindranath Tagore and Kazi Nazrul Islam are being challenged due to ongoing Islamisation (McDermott 2012, 295). The author criticises the general approach to depicting Bangladeshi women as victims of patriarchy and, at the same time, defends the role of Bangladeshi women by saying that many women live a choice-based life and contribute to the cultural propaganda of the nation (Schendel 2009, 34). Schendel draws on mythology and history to reinvestigate the role of women born or thought to be born in ancient Bengal who contributed a lot to the progress of Bengali civilisation. These Bengali women, such as Behula[5] and Begum Rokeya,[6] have challenged traditional patriarchal roles throughout the ages and inspired Bengali women to fight against the threats in their way. Schendel's book not only focuses on women's multifaceted roles in the Liberation War but also investigates how Bangladeshi women have always raised their voices to maintain the secular spirit in post-war Bangladesh (2009, 208).

Willem van Schendel's book is important to read the gender issues of the 1971 war for it blends historical narratives with literary narratives to cite examples of the women in the 1971 war from literature (2009). While locating women in the 1971 conflict, Schendel's historical account emphasises the literary narratives of the Bangladeshi writers whose songs, poetry and novels speak of the war. One such instance is his allusion to the poem of Sufia Kamal (1911–1999), an eminent literary figure and war diarist. In her poem 'No More Time for Braiding your Hair', Sufia Kamal urges the women in Bangladesh to break stereotypes for the nation's sake.

> There's no more time for braiding your hair in patterns,
> Or for being concerned with the glamorous border of your saris,
> The tip mark on your forehead, your mascara or lipstick.
> No more time, no more time—for the battle for life is on!
> The women have shed their coy, delicate gentility
> To wreak vengeance for the sorrow of their lost dear ones.
> In their slender bodies and hearts is gathered
> The courage of lions.
> Boundless strength they hold—these valiant women.
> (quoted in Schendel 2009, 165)

Schendel's book is an imperative contribution to the studies of the historiography of the 1971 war because it also provides more space for gender issues than the accounts of the South Asian historians. His portrayal of the Birangona after the war is quite broad and analytical. His observation of the lives of those rape survivors aligns with the narratives of Neelima Ibrahim and Nayanika Mookherjee. Like Ibrahim, Schendel also acknowledges that the State has failed to provide the honour due to these brave girls and their war babies. Their condition has worsened again despite the State's initiative to relocate them into mainstream society (Schendel 2009, 173).

Why Feminist Intervention Is Required

The earlier discussion makes it evident that women's victimisation and their agency in war and war resolution processes in the context of the Liberation War of Bangladesh have been largely ignored by Bangladeshi historians as well as by the historians of the subcontinent. Hence, a feminist intervention is necessary to fill the gaps because the recent emergence of women's narratives in fiction, non-fiction and press articles has unearthed many instances of women's engagement in the 1971 war. 'Each time a girl opens a book and reads a womanless history, she learns she is worthless' (Sadkar n.d.). This degraded position of women in the history of the 1971 war was challenged by contemporary feminist writers and activists who observed that even fifty years after the 1971 war, a large section of people in Bangladesh still think it is shameful to bring the rape survivors to the fore. In countries like Bangladesh, the public exposure of rape is considered a taboo. While the rest of the world now considers rape a criminal act, in Bangladesh, it is still considered a crime against the personal dignity of women rather than a crime against humanity (Linton 2010b, 239). Gendered issues like rape and the survival of the rape victims are represented in the history of Bangladesh in the same way as in public consciousness. The importance of rereading the narratives of the women in the 1971 war is that it not only changes history from being gender-biased to gender-sensitive but also inspires other women, especially in South Asian regions, to come forward and tell the untold stories of the past. In the words of Yasmin Saikia:

> Shining a spotlight on the 1971 war and incorporating its documentation from the lived experience of people may move us closer to creating a broader template of war memories, and writing an inclusive story of the remembered and the forgotten to begin the process of knowing the shared condition of humanity, within and outside Bangladesh. (Saikia 2011b, 242)

Women play mainly three roles in wars: as victims, as nurses of wounded soldiers and, finally, as fighters. Throughout war history, women have been mostly shown in the first role, that is, as victims of war, and their roles as saviours and fighters have been overlooked. War history shows that their victimisation through rape is a common tactic. The dominating group of soldiers exploits the women of the weaker section during the war. Rape, therefore, has not only been weaponised in ethnic conflicts but also initiated and practised in every type of war in world history. The victorious soldiers use rape to inflict shame not only on female bodies but also on the minds of their male counterparts who were unable to save their honour (Cook 2006, xxxi). Employed as a vital weapon, rape was a layered tool to subjugate the enemy by morally degrading the community in several wars, such as in the civil wars in Cambodia, Kosovo and Rwanda, the France-Algeria war and the Second World War. During the Second World War, women from poor and downtrodden families in the areas occupied by the Japanese army were forced to prostitute themselves to the soldiers under the tag of 'comfort women' (112). Rape has emerged as an effective weapon in ethnic cleansing. In Bosnia, 20,000 Muslim girls and women have been raped since the beginning of the ethnic struggle in the country (UNICEF n.d.).

During the 1971 war in Bangladesh, rape was an important mechanism to mediate the ethnic struggle between the Bengali and the Urdu community, which was well documented in academic works and media throughout the world. Amidst the accusations that Pakistan has attempted to hide the facts and that Bangladesh has exaggerated the intensity of the victimisation, there are ample references from international volunteers and media persons that suggest that women were raped to morally degrade the Bengali community. Bangladeshi sources often claim that almost three million people were brutally killed, one million people migrated to India as refugees and 200,000 to 400,000 women were raped followed by the pregnancy of 25,000 women (Linton 2010b, 194). However, the report of the Pakistani judicial commission dismisses Bangladesh's estimate of the figures of raped women as a 'fantastical exaggeration' and asserts that not more than 26,000 East Pakistani people were killed (202). Sarmila Bose also supports Pakistan's claim of exaggeration, and she says that Bangladesh's claim about the number of casualties and rape victims is 'pure fabrication' (2011a, 164). However, the claims made by people who were actively engaged in the war and the rehabilitation process in the aftermath mostly support the numbers put forward by Bangladeshis. Dr Geoffrey Davis, in an interview with Bina D'Costa, dismisses Pakistan's and Sarmila Bose's theory of exaggeration (2011). Davis, a medical graduate from Sydney, was appointed as a specialist doctor in Bangladesh in 1972 for the mass abortion process of the rape survivors of the war. According to him, the number presented by Bangladesh is very conservative compared to the damage done by the Pakistani military in Bangladesh (D'Costa 2011, 197). Pakistan's government restricted the freedom of the press while the genocide happened. Almost all international journalists were forced to leave Dhaka. Figuring out the intensity of the violence is problematic unless we take help from the people who were directly associated with it. Lisa Curtis, a research fellow at the Heritage Foundation, says, 'Regardless of what the number is, clearly massive atrocities took place against the Bengali people.… I think we have to say that the atrocities committed by the Pakistan military far outstripped what we saw from the other side' (quoted in Boissoneault 2016).

The portrayal of women as rape victims is very common in war history, but it is difficult to come across instances of women's agency in wartime and their roles as saviours, fighters and policy makers. Primarily, this omission is due to the politics involved in the representation of women by male authors who construct history in their texts. Such representation of women was criticised by Virginia Woolf[7] when she validated the need for the feminist lens as an ideological weapon to create participation, if not dominance. Despite such neglect in the pages of history, women's contribution to all the major wars in the world not only as nurses in hospitals or inspirers in houses but also as fighters in the war is praiseworthy. During the Second World War, Soviet women participated on a large scale in the armed conflict (Cook 2006, 543). In the context of South Asia also, women have contributed to wars and ethnic struggles like the Liberation War of Bangladesh of 1971, the civil war in Sri Lanka (1983–2009), the Kashmir insurgency (1989–present), the insurgency in North-East India (1954–present) and the like.

The Bangladeshi women's contributions as fighters in the resistance, though neglected by the main course of historiography, is evident and proven as per recent academic research and media investigation. There are plenty of instances available in narratives and media portrayals to show that women have had the power of defence over male authority. Neelima Ibrahim documented the stories of resistance and courage of seven women who experienced sexual violence during the Liberation War in her 1994 book *Aami Birangona Balchi* (A War Heroine, I Speak). These Birangona of the 1971 war did not yield to the subjugation of the patriarchal society, and they defied various stereotypes. The survival story of Rama Chowdhury (1936–2018), a Birangona in post-war Bangladesh, shows up the world how women can be courageous and valiant and resist the torture, subjugation and stereotypes of a patriarchal society. Rama was brutally raped and mentally tortured by the Pakistani military during the war, and she lost three of her children in the same war. After the end of the war, she did not succumb to the situation. Instead, she documented her stories of survival and sacrifice in eighteen published books. Popularly known as *Ekattorer Janani* (mother of 1971), she had no one in her life to whom she could tell her stories of pain and suffering. Even the people of Bangladesh failed to give her due respect in her lifetime (Huda 2018). Rama Chowdhury never exhibited her books or sold them for commercial purposes. Instead, she went door to door, selling her books to enrich the modern generation with the narratives of the people of the 1971 war and the pain inflicted on the mothers who lost their children in the violence (Karim 2018). She continues to be a role model for women's empowerment in Bengal because she was amongst the very few women in the 1960s who had a master's degree (in Bengali language and literature). She was a teacher before her ordeal (Huda 2018). Such accounts of women who contributed a lot to the formation of the new nation of Bangladesh is surprisingly missing from the history of the nation.

Reframing History: Women's Victimhood and Resistance in Narratives

As the history of the Liberation War is fragmented, incomplete and fabricated to an extent, much scholarly intervention is essential to reframe the facts and numbers related to the death toll and rape victims. The lacunae in history are acknowledged by many Bangladeshi academicians and international writers. Most historians have not followed a systematic process to record the narratives of the people who were directly associated with the war, and hence, the historiography appears to be fragmented and interrupted (Hossain 2006). Feminist historiography, which is mainly in the modes of narratives or storytelling, has tried to solve this incompleteness. Based on the successive narratives of victims and press reports after the war, a large number of women were assumed to have been sexually victimised during the war (Mookherjee 2015b, 133). The importance of feminist historiography is that it reads women's experiences at multiple levels that are impossible for traditional historiography. For instance, Neelima Ibrahim (2017), Bina D'Costa (2011) and Nayanika Mookherjee (2015b) have endeavoured to show the trajectories of the Bengali rape survivors of the 1971 war, their survival strategies, their subjugation through dislocation and migration and so on. On the other hand, Yasmin Saikia has broadly focused on a completely different side: the victimisation of Bihari women by the Bengali nationalists as revenge. Overall, these oral histories, which are directly derived from the voices of the victims, can work as a supplement to the existing history of women and 'can give a texture and quality to women's lives' (Mookherjee 2015b, 11).

Nowadays, women's resistance against power and domination and its relation to their victimhood is a subject of immense concern and study in academia. Many women who were victims in the war emerged as tough fighters in their later lives. 'After overcoming feelings of blame or shame and beliefs that they deserved abuse and violence, women begin to regain a sense of self and their own humanity' (McFadden 2014). Though the historiographies failed to represent women's resilience in the war, post-war narratives by South Asian women emphasised it through the portrayal of women activists and victims in the war. Women's agency in the war is reflected in two types of narratives: fictional narratives based on the real-life experiences of women and narrative non-fiction related to women's direct life experiences in the forms of interviews and memoirs. Women's courageous deeds during the war and in its aftermath have also been portrayed in many media representations in post-war Bangladesh. When historical representations at multiple levels fail to recognise women's individuality and their unique roles in the war, post-war narratives by many feminist academicians reinvestigated their roles. A.M. Amin, L.A. Ahmed, and S. Ahsan narrate the story of Taramon Bibi, a woman who directly fought in the armed conflict in the 1971 war but remained invisible even in the official account of Bangladesh's war history. She fought the war in her village, Shankar Madhabpur, in Kurigram District of Bangladesh in Sector 11, under the leadership of Sector Commander Abu Taher. She remained discreet after the end of the war, and her story came to light due to the initiative of a Bangladeshi researcher. Her story of bravery gained recognition, and she was awarded the title 'Bir

Pratik'[8] by the Government of Bangladesh in 1995 (Amin et al. 2016)

The efforts of Pakistani historians to suppress the brutality inflicted on the people of Bangladesh in 1971 turned futile even in Pakistan due to the emerging narratives by the successive generation. The question of whether political representation in history can detach the common people's consciousness from the memory of war is a significant one. The answer is certainly a big 'no' because literary and non-literary narratives over the decades by Pakistani writers and media persons have led to a reinvestigation of the crimes against humanity committed in the 1971 war. The first evidence-based article about the violence appeared in international media with Pakistani journalist Anthony Mascarenhas's article 'Genocide'. The article appeared in the United Kingdom's *Sunday Times* on 13 June 1971, describing the mass murder in Bangladesh. The article compelled the diplomats of the world to exert pressure on Pakistan and also helped Indira Gandhi to chalk out India's diplomatic mission to assist Bangladesh in gaining their freedom. Mascarenhas starts with a brave representation of the brutality:

> Abdul Bari had run out of luck. Like thousands of other people in East Bengal, he had made the mistake—the fatal mistake—of running within sight of a Pakistani patrol. He was 24 years old, a slight man surrounded by soldiers. He was trembling because he was about to be shot. (Dummett 2011)

The Pakistani intelligentsia seems to be divided in their ideological position on the 1971 war. While one group is mainly historians and political persons who have tried to suppress the history of gendered violence and genocide over the decades, the other group feels solidarity with the victims of the war. The number of people in the second group is not few. Recent blog posts, newspaper articles and literary narratives by prominent Pakistani writers such as Kamila Shamsie (2002) and Sorayya Khan (2004) acknowledge that the Pakistani army committed horrific gender crimes in the 1971 war against Bangladesh. Kamila Shamsie, a Pakistani diasporic writer, has shared the modern Pakistani people's consciousness of the rape and genocide perpetrated by Pakistani soldiers in the 1971 war in her novel *Kartography* (2002). The novel is a haunting memory of betrayal, sacrifice, suffering and despair for women like the protagonist Karim's Bengali mother, whose memory transcends generations and influences their lives too (Lezard 2003). A.U. Qasmi, a writer and an assistant professor of history at the Lahore University of Management Sciences, Pakistan, wrote an article, '1971 War: Witness to History' (published in February 2017), to pinpoint the politics in the historical representation of the events of the 1971 war in Pakistan as well as in Bangladesh. Unlike traditional Pakistani historians, Qasmi feels ashamed while travelling in Bangladesh when he observes the memories of the brutality of the war scattered throughout the country. His simple acknowledgement justifies the stand of many intellectuals in Pakistan:

> As a Pakistani, I felt remorse, guilt and shame every time I walked into the corridors of Dhaka University. The names of the students, intellectuals and teachers, who died as a result of Pakistani military actions in March to December 1971, are prominently displayed. A number of other historical sites are also located on the campus or situated close by. (Qasmi 2017)

Qasmi also acknowledges that thousands of Bengali women were raped by the Pakistani military force during the nine-month-long war, and they had to live miserably after the war due to social marginalisation for being raped and carrying war babies. International non-governmental organisations (NGOs) and medical practitioners volunteered to help in the process of the abortion and adoption of war babies after the war (Qasmi 2017). Qasmi alleges that the historical accounts by both countries are fabricated. According to him, Bangladesh exaggerated the number of deaths and raped women to seek international attention, and Pakistan, at the same time, wanted to keep the number of deaths in the genocide below one million (Qasmi 2017).

Feminist narratives also unearth the injustice done to the non-Bengali women in the 1971 war. When the main course of historiography avoided it to an extent, the victims' narratives brought forth by Sarmila Bose and Yasmin Saikia opened a new horizon in genocide research in South Asia by highlighting the Bihari women who had been victimised as revenge. Saikia asserts that both ethnic groups, Urdu-speaking Pakistanis and Bengali-speaking Bangladeshis, behaved irrationally in a misplaced sense of nationalism and engaged in horrific crimes like raping women (2004, 286).

Conclusion

When historical representation appears to be gendered as well as conflicting and, at times, seems fabricated, the post-structural approach to historical studies tends to disfigure history through narratives. At least it would bring relativity to the studies of historiography because narratives are concerned with human experiences that can never be the same. Hayden White discusses the role of narratives in studying history when history fails to show the truth:

> Far from being a problem, then, narrative might well be considered a solution to a problem of general human concern, namely, the problem of how to translate *knowing* into *telling*, the problem of fashioning human experience into a form assimilable to structures of meaning that are generally human rather than culture-specific. (1980, 5)

With the emergence of postmodernism, including feminism, post-structuralism, queer theory and critical race theory, the traditional genres of writing have been challenged. At the same time, the genre of ethnography has been blurred, extended and elaborated with different types of formats and approaches of research writing (Richardson and Pierre 2018, 1414–1415). Feminist ethnography is a postmodern approach to ethnographic research and writing that challenges the traditional versions of truth in historical writings with a more relative and contextual approach to it with its detailed interventions in gender issues. As a method, it takes the readers' consciousness beyond the traditional androcentric and Eurocentric approaches (Ghosh 2016, 1). Feminist ethnographic narratives play a vital role in the studies of the history of women in the 1971 war because an extensive literature review makes it clear that history has failed to recognise the contribution of its women in most cases. The approach of listening and engaging with the narratives of women in the South Asian context would bring a post-structural approach to historiography through the decolonising tradition of male narratives in history (Saikia 2011b, 242). The intention of complementing history with narratives in the context of the Liberation War of Bangladesh started in 1994 with Neelima Ibrahim's book, *Aami Birangona Balchi*. Thereafter, the narratives of more victims and activists of the Liberation War appeared through South Asian and international feminist writers such as Tahmima Anam, Nayanika Mookherjee, Yasmin Saikia, Sarmila Bose and many others. These narratives reveal the survival strategies of the women who survived the 1971 war.

Before the arrival of these feminist ethnographic narratives, women were reluctant to expose themselves, their untold stories of contribution to this society and their stories of the pain they had endured. However, the emergence of their subaltern voice through narratives has proven Spivak's words that subaltern women can overcome every threat and the politics of patriarchal representation if they get a proper chance (Spivak 1988, 25). The emergence of the narrative voice of the women of the 1971 war also compelled many perpetrators to come under the purview of transnational justice. The journey was full of hurdles, and the women had to strive a lot to establish their voice. The narratives of these subaltern voices played a crucial role in the International Crimes Tribunal in Bangladesh set up in 2012 to prosecute Razakars. The gradual emergence of women's voices in narratives to reframe the gendered historiography of the 1971 war will inspire women of other regions of South Asia and beyond to bring forth their hidden narratives.

Notes

1 Geneva Camp is a camp in Dhaka, Bangladesh, occupied by the stateless Bihari people who migrated to Bangladesh after the Partition and collaborated with the Pakistani government in the 1971 war. They became stranded in the camp because after the creation of Bangladesh, the Pakistani government refused to take them back. See Report (2018).

2 Mujibnagar was the provisional Government of Bangladesh that was set up in April 1971 during the Liberation War as an initiative to support the freedom fighters to raise funds, seek international attention and monitor the war.

3 The day of the Pakistani military's surrender to the allied forces of the Bangladeshi Muktibahini and the Indian Army on 16 December 1971 is commemorated by celebrating 16 December as Victory Day every year in Bangladesh. Bangladesh celebrates their Independence Day and Victory Day separately. The former is celebrated on 26 March to remember the day in 1971 when Sheikh Mujibur Rahman declared independence from Pakistani rule.

4 Ayub Khan was a military leader who became the president of Pakistan.

5 Behula is a legendary woman who appears in the *Shiva Purana* and the *Manashamangala*, two Hindu religious scriptures. She was believed to have been born in Bengal and is famous for actively arguing with the gods and goddesses to save her husband's life. She is a symbol of an anti-patriarchal voice of female resistance.

6 Begum Rokeya was a Bengali feminist thinker born in Rangpur District of Bangladesh. She endeavoured to contribute to women's empowerment and women's education in South Asia during British rule.

7 Virginia Woolf, a noted feminist of the 20th century, criticised men's authority in historiography in her feminist book *A Room of One's Own* (1929).

8 'Bir Pratik' is one of the prestigious titles conferred on valiant freedom fighters in Bangladesh by the Government of Bangladesh.

3

Women of the 1971 War in Fictional Narratives

> The only reason for the existence of a novel is that it does attempt to represent life ... as the picture is reality, so the novel is history.
>
> —H. James, 'The Art of Fiction'

Introduction

In the previous chapter, various historical sources from the Liberation War were discussed to clarify that history has scarcely dealt with women's positive agency in the war and has stereotyped them as victims. War literature has always been a vital resource to unearth many hidden stories associated with war in global contexts. While history deals with factual events, many regular happenings in the lives of common people against the backdrop of war are largely ignored, especially when it comes to women's roles and their agency. The gendered nature of history is apparent in the historiography of the 1971 war too. On the other hand, both fictional and non-fictional narratives of the war have revealed many hidden truths about women's involvement in the war as not only victims but also diplomats, fighters and bearers of memory and trauma. Literary narratives, mostly by women, show women's connection with the ethnic struggle and their marginalisation through the ethnic politics of their men. Contemporary feminist writers and ethnographers of South Asia have observed the lives of the women in this region and traced their stories of suffering, bravery and solidarity. They have then compiled those stories into fictional and non-fictional narratives. To emphasise the role of literature in showing the truth of violence, Chaity Das says, '[Literature] not only provides a bridge between memory and history by allowing for euphoria, melancholy, and mourning, it re-presents violence—its gut-wrenching and at times cathartic spectacularly, the experience of terror, shame, humiliation, victory, defeat, and annihilation' (2017, Preface, Para 1).

The end of the 20th century and the beginning of the 21st century saw the rise of novels dealing with South Asian wars and conflicts. Several novels from South Asia and its diaspora that dealt directly and indirectly with the 1971 war were published. Salman Rushdie's Booker Prize-winning novel *Midnight's Children* is one such novel that includes the war as an extended backdrop to the Partition. The novel indirectly alludes to Indira Gandhi's intervention in the war and the Hindu–Muslim chaos in the Pakistani and Indian armies, which was followed by the sterilisation camp and Indira Gandhi's defeat in the successive election ([1981] 2013). His next novel, *Shame*, also refers to the 1971 war and harshly criticises West Pakistan's looting of the resources of East Pakistan and their imposed dictatorship there ([1983] 2008, 13). The 1971 war has been a major theme in Bangladeshi literature and visual narratives since the end of the war and Bangladesh's achievement of long-cherished independence. Nayanika Mookherjee has written about some novels set in 1970s Bangladesh such as two of Neelima Ibrahim's works that were published in 1974—*Je Oronne Alo Nei* (The forest which has no light) and *Lal Golap Dojoke* (Red rose in hell) (2015b). These novels by Ibrahim gave the Birangona a much-needed voice when the emergence of Bengali nationalism and the military government overlooked the history of the sexual violence experienced by women in the 1971 war (Mookherjee 2015b, 207). Well-known Bangladeshi contemporary novelist Anisul Hoque documented the life of the famous Bangladeshi freedom fighter Magfar Ahmed Chowdhury (nicknamed Azad) in his novel *Freedom's Mother* (2012). The novel depicts the brutal death of Azad, a student of the University of Dhaka, his mother Safia's journey to find his body and her death from hunger and poverty.

At the beginning of the 20th century, a few novels dealing with the gender issues of the 1971 war were written by acclaimed scholars and anthropologists not only from Bangladesh but also from South Asia and its diaspora. These novels are not merely a fictional representation of the lives of people in the context of the war. Instead, the novelists have conducted an ethnographic intervention and sincere observation of the lives of women who were essential parts of the 1971 war and whose survival stories and vital agency have been neglected in the pages of history. Dilruba Z. Ara's *Blame* (2015), Tahmima Anam's *A Golden Age* (2007) and Kamila Shamsie's *Kartography* (2002) are among those novels that can be termed feminist ethnographic novels because the novelists have taken a postmodern approach to cross the barriers between anthropology and fiction. Derived from anthropology and cultural studies, feminist ethnography challenges the prolonged politics of representation of women's voices in male-controlled historiography, giving a voice to the voiceless (Aune 2009, 330). While discussing the connection of anthropology to literary genres such as the autobiography and the novel, Kamala Visweswaran rightly quotes Marcel Mauss: '[An] anthropologist has to be also a novelist able to evoke the life of a whole society' (1994, 16). When the patriarchal nature of history suppresses women's voices in the pages of history, a feminist ethnographic endeavour can do justice by providing various insights about women's involvement in the war, their stories as victims and their agency. Though ethnographic literature is mostly non-fictional and is supposed to provide accurate narratives, the postmodern approach has reframed this nature of ethnography and ensured that it can exist as 'creative nonfiction; fiction; ethnographic fiction; the nonfiction novel; and true fiction' (Richardson 2000, 253).

The present chapter chooses three novels for analysis: Dilruba Z. Ara's *Blame* (2015), Tahmima Anam's *A Golden Age* (2007) and Kamila

Shamsie's *Kartography* (2002), three feminist fictional narratives on the 1971 war in Bangladesh by three writers who have a broad geopolitical experience of the region and who conducted a sincere observation of women's lives before writing these novels. First, women's stereotypical roles in the history of 1971 as victims and agents of blame are re-evaluated by aligning them with Dilruba Z. Ara's depiction of women in *Blame* (2015). Second, women's involvement in the war, which has been neglected in traditional historiography, is discussed in Tahmima Anam's novel *A Golden Age* (2007). Third, women's marginalisation in the 1971 war's ethnic struggle and the formation of their cartography based on their struggle is discussed with an illustration from Kamila Shamsie's *Kartography* (2002). Finally, the conclusion discusses how these representations offer fresh perspectives on women's roles and their agency in connection with the 1971 war in Bangladesh. Due to the limited scope of this book, some novels that have contributed a lot to re-registering the female voice in the archives of Bangladesh could not be discussed here. *The Good Muslim*, the second novel in Tahmima Anam's Bengal trilogy and the sequel to her previous novel *The Golden Age*, also carries forward the legacy of the Liberation War (2011). The book shows the degradation of the secular spirit of Bangladesh by describing the character Sohail's transformation from a spirited freedom fighter to a prospective religious leader. Set in the 1980s when the country was under military dictatorship, this novel criticises Bangladesh's failure to protect the spirit of the *Muktijuddha* (the Liberation War) and its gradual conversion into an orthodox country that did not glorify the deeds of the women who participated in the freedom struggle and marginalised them through social stigmas. Shaheen Akhtar, another Bangladeshi author, highlights women's degraded conditions in the post-conflict era of the country in her novel *Taalash* (2006). The methodology of this research firstly discusses whether the fictional works chosen for this chapter are feminist ethnographic texts. Then, these novels are evaluated based on Richardson's matrixes of evaluating ethnography (2000).

Women as Agents of Blame

Contemporary studies of the 1971 Liberation War of Bangladesh by South Asian female writers have ignited a reinvestigation of the intensity of violence and rape and attribution of blame. Ethnicity-based gendered violence in 1971 and the sudden shift in the attribution of the blame are some of the issues that have also been dealt with by a few Bangladeshi diasporic novelists such as Tahmima Anam and Dilruba Z. Ara in their post-2000 novels written in English. Dilruba Z. Ara, a Swedish-Bangladeshi novelist, emphasises that the blame game is a significant repercussion of war in her novel *Blame* (2015). Ara clarifies that the Bengali people blamed Pakistanis for the 1971 genocide whereas Pakistanis blamed Bengali nationalists for not abiding by the nationality of Pakistan. This novel, in the form of a Bildungsroman, is divided into three parts that narrate the female protagonist's journey from the bondage of patriarchy to a liberal life, her engagement in the war and her sexual victimisation in the same war. The mass killing of civilians, the plundering of the country and the victimisation of women do not end with the war. The blame game continues during the war resolution process. Courageous women such as Ara's protagonist Laila and her friend Gita are blamed for their victimisation. Ara's tradition of fiction writing is based on her personal experience in the war. The novel is a heart-wrenching tale of the 'unsung heroines' of the 1971 war, as mentioned by the author in an interview with the *Dhaka Tribune*. Dilruba Z. Ara acknowledges her feminist ethnographic endeavour behind the novel. She says:

> *Blame* is based on my personal experience. Though some parts are fictional, most of the characters are drawn from real life, so the story is more or less true.... For me, the important things are how the Bangladeshi psyche was formed, and the role played by the Bangladeshi women during the liberation war. It's time we spoke of those unsung heroines of Bangladesh. (Haque 2016)

So, Ara's acknowledgement ensures that the novel is grounded in the sociopolitical context of the war and its atrocities and that the author's consciousness and exposure to the 1971 war were connected with her writing. Laila, the protagonist, represents the women of 1970s Bangladesh who defied patriarchal decorum and religious orthodoxy to engage in the nation's struggle for independence. Her involvement with student politics, affair with her Hindu neighbour Santo and association with her Hindu neighbour Gita in the freedom movement reflect the secular spirit of Bangladeshi women who equally contributed to the struggle but always remained outcasts in the official history of independent Bangladesh. Ara shows that the blame game is a crucial part of the war game, with an analogy between politics and fiction. The novel's narratives merge with the historical narratives of political movements in 1960s Pakistan and the formation of independent Bangladesh in 1971. Blame is assigned in the novel on various occasions: West Pakistanis and pro-Pakistanis were blamed for their role in the genocide and gendered violence. Bengalis, on the other hand, were blamed for being traitorous to the nationality and integrity of Pakistan. Biharis were blamed for their ethnic connection to Urdu and their collaboration with the Pakistanis due to that connection. They suffered from an existential crisis amidst the confusion of the war game and the blame game, switching frequently between the two games. If war is considered a crucial game, blame is a game as well (Mortuza 2016). In the same context, this section discusses Ara's approach to the blame game being a direct result of the war game. For the theoretical framework, this section broadly follows the 'Theory of Blame' propounded by Bertram F. Malle, S. Guglielmo and A.E. Monroe (2014).

Divided into three parts, '1965', '1968–1969' and '1970–1971', the novel has a prologue titled '1971' and an epilogue titled 'Afterwards'. In the prologue, the characters of the novel are trapped in the main water body of their native land amidst the corpses of other Bengali men as well as naked Bengali women who were thrown in the river after being raped. Horrific violence pervades the land in the sense that the war is not just a political event. The violence percolates down to day-to-day life where even nature becomes a witness to it. Ara writes, 'East Bengal soil is rich with winding rivers, but these days the waterways too had become a battlefield, where fish-mouths carried the stain of human blood, as vultures' beaks did in the sky' (2015, 1). The historical narratives of Bangladesh claim that at least three million people were brutally killed, and 200,000 to 400,000 women were raped during the nine-month freedom struggle in Bangladesh (Linton 2010b, 194). The novel echoes that brutality by narrating a few incidents of the war.

The first part of the novel is a flashback to the days of the political turmoil in East Pakistan in 1965. The third-person narrator introduces Laila, the eldest daughter of a Kazi family living in Chandgaon near Chittagong, a port city in East Pakistan (which later became Bangladesh in 1971). Laila's childhood memories are characterised by her friendship with a Hindu girl, Gita, and Laila's infatuation with Gita's brother, Santo. Her father, Harun Kazi, and her uncle Khaled Kazi believe in a united Pakistan, and they despise the Bengalis who are actively involved in fanning the flames of Bengali nationalism. Bengali people are referred to as 'infidels' by the pro-Pakistanis for not supporting the idea of the national integrity of Pakistan and are urged to form a brotherhood based not on ethnicity but on religion (Ara 2015, 36–37). Gopal, Shikha and their daughter Gita suffer from an identity crisis because they are Hindus in a country where they are not wanted (37). This part ends with the political blame put on West Pakistan, followed by criticism of the prolonged sociopolitical prejudices by West Pakistanis towards the people of East Pakistan.

The second part of the novel (1968–1969) focuses on East Pakistan's journey towards a civil war based on ethnic issues. The narrative skips three years, and in the meantime, Santo's family has moved to Dhaka where his father works as a clerk at Eden College. Laila insists that her parents let her pursue higher studies after completing her secondary school examinations, but her parents think that it is unsuitable for a Kazi girl to follow a path that will take her outside the domestic space (Ara 2015, 46). After being supported by Aunt Mili and Alam Khan (Laila's would-be father-in-law), Laila succeeds in migrating from Chandgaon to Dhaka for higher education. At first, Laila lives in Alam Khan's Kalabagan residence in Dhaka where she finds Khan's wife, her aunt Salma Khan, as orthodox as her parents. Nila, the fourteen-year-old daughter of Alam Khan, is friendly with Laila, who has the support of Alam Khan and Kamil (Laila's would-be brother-in-law). The communal tension between Hindus and Muslims since the Partition of 1947 is highlighted in this section (63). Later, Laila moves to the ladies' hostel. There, she, along with other girls such as Rashida and Camilla, espouses revolutionary ideas. The artist Amzad Haq's house becomes the den of the revolutionaries, and Laila joins the group with Santo, Gita, Kamil and Jamil. Professor Merina supports the girls and forms a secret revolutionary group with them. The country's youngsters unite against the prolonged discrimination by the West Pakistani government.

The third part, titled '1970–1971' (Ara 2015, 139–366) is the longest and most important section of the novel. The characters find that politics and personal relationships start to intertwine. Laila's infatuation with Santo develops into love, and Jamil, despite following the same track as Laila and Santo, experiences an identity crisis. In the political sphere, Sheikh Mujib gets the support of all East Pakistanis and wins the parliamentary elections of 1970 with a landslide majority (160). After Mujib's big win in the election, the Pakistan government intensifies their repressive measures against the Bengali people in East Pakistan. Therefore, Mujib declares the independence of Bangladesh in a historic speech on 7 March 1971 and urges his people to defend the land at all costs, including the possibility of fighting a war against the West Pakistani army (167). Though the 1971 war has been labelled as a liberation war, it has the characteristics of a civil war. It was a civil war not only because the eastern wing of Pakistan was engaged in a war against the organised government of Pakistan but also because it was a war between the supporters of a united Pakistan, on one hand, and independent Bangladesh, on the other (Hannan 2007). When the war breaks out, Laila's and Santo's families move from Dhaka to Chittagong (141–142), and then to Potaya and many other places like refugees, imprisoned and abandoned in their own country (175–366). Santo, Jamil, Kamil and Jadu join the freedom struggle. Jamil works as an undercover agent to spy on the Pakistani soldiers because he knows Urdu well. Laila, unable to just sit back and tolerate the violence, joins the freedom struggle along with Gita. When the military troops find the sanctuary of Laila's family, they kill Laila's father and arrest her for killing one of her father's torturers. She is then taken to the military camp and sexually assaulted there. Jamil collaborates with Yousef, a pro-Pakistani, to free Laila in exchange for Gita. Jamil is blamed by Laila, Santo and other freedom fighters who suspect him of collaborating with the pro-Pakistanis. Gita is rescued in a valiant mission performed by Santo, Kamil, Jamil, Laila and a group of freedom fighters, but she has already endured all sorts of ordeals and sexual abuse during her stay in the camp. Kamil and Santo never return from the campaign and are later found dead. Though Laila and Gita seek shelter in Alam Khan's house, almost everyone continually blames them for being 'polluted'. The Bengalis of East Pakistan attain their cherished freedom. They find a new homeland for themselves, which they had dreamt of for so long, thanks to the direct intervention of India that leads to the end of the war. However, the sufferings of Laila and Gita do not end as they are disowned by their families. Ostracised, they take shelter at a rehabilitation centre. Gita gives birth to a child, which is later adopted by a Canadian couple.

The epilogue of the novel shows Laila and Gita in a new kind of struggle. They have been trained at the centre, after which Laila has found a job as a secretary and Gita has become a school teacher. The narrative voice shifts from the third person to the first person. The author shifts her narrative voice from the 1970s to her contemporary time. She now speaks for thousands of Gitas and Lailas who continue to be victimised across South Asia but who did not speak up because 'the girls must remain silent' (Ara 2015, 368). In a patriarchal society like Bangladesh, as Yasmin Saikia states, the women's role is to remain oblivious to the violence perpetrated upon them, and if they are unable to do so, they might be charged with adultery (2011b, 91).

Cognitive blame and social blame are the two sides of blame. Cognitive blame is constructed from properties inherited from social blame (Malle et al. 2014, 148). Regarding the formation of the consciousness of the Bangladeshi people about the 1971 war, Yasmin Saikia claims that one-sided historiography only paints Pakistanis as 'evil' and Bangladeshis as 'good,' along with an extreme glorification of the Muktibahini (2004, 277). The Bangladeshi psyche has thus already become habituated to the assigning of social blame against Pakistanis as perpetrators of violence during the civil war in 1971. The formation of cognitive blame from social blame in the Bangladeshi psyche is apparent in Ara's *Blame* (2015). The novel epitomises blame at various levels against the then Pakistani government by the East Pakistani people, drawing references from different contemporary social and political issues. Though blame and anger share some common features, the two should not be fused. Anger can end without blaming while blaming can happen without anger (Malle et al. 2014, 149). *Blame* shows the display of anger followed by blame and vice versa. The common people of East Pakistan were angry at West Pakistan for exploiting the labour and resources of the eastern region for their security as well as political and financial gain. Blame and counter-blame between East and West Pakistan go on throughout the novel in the context of the 1960s and 1970s. Sheikh Mujibur Rahman, the East Pakistani leader, demanded autonomy for East Pakistan. So he was imprisoned in the Agartala Conspiracy Case, which was a hoax aimed at disarming him (Ara 2015, 89). Some prominent West Pakistani leaders, such as Ayub Khan, Yahya Khan and Tikka Khan (1915–2002), were accused of depriving East Pakistani people of their rights. In *Blame*, the narrator remarks, 'They left us totally defenceless, to fight this lost battle over Kashmir with money from our jute and fishing industries' (2015, 40). Kashmir, which is politically divided into Indian-administered Jammu and Kashmir and Pakistan-administered Azad Kashmir, has remained a contentious zone between India and Pakistan since the Partition of 1947. India and Pakistan have fought several wars over their right to Kashmir, the world's highest battlefield at an altitude of 20,000 feet (Qazi 2016, 18).

Social blame is employed to regulate the agent's behaviour by devaluing and criticising his or her violation of the norm. Social blame is contingent upon time and context. Generally, the society or a community decides who will be blamed by whom and for what (Malle et al. 2014, 171). In the book *Blame*, the social blame put forward by the common people, the intellectuals and the politicians of East Pakistan turns out to be fruitful in a few cases. It manages to change the behaviour and motives of the West Pakistani rulers. The novel shows the effect of social blame on the politics of Pakistan at various levels. Sheikh Mujib was acquitted unconditionally in the Agartala Conspiracy Case, and Ayub Khan handed over power to the then army chief Mohammad Yahya Khan who declared general elections in December 1970 (Ara 2015, 137–138). Upon realising the extent of support that Mujib had in those days, Yahya Khan called for a tri-party convention to discuss the prospect of a National Assembly (160). Sheikh Mujib won against his Pakistani opponent in the National Assembly, and he expected to be given the post of prime minister (164). However, the Pakistani government appeared rather hesitant about handing over power to Mujib, which resulted in violence among the people in East Pakistan. Here, blame, as suggested in the theory of the blame game, appears to follow anger (Malle et al. 2014, 149). The East Pakistanis set fire to the properties of West Pakistanis, harassed the non-Bengalis and shouted slogans against the Pakistani government (164). Sheikh Mujib's speech at the Dhaka Racecourse ground on

7 March 1971 inspired the youngsters to shed their blood for the sake of a nation of their own: 'Our struggle this time is a struggle for freedom, our struggle this time is a struggle for independence, Joi Bangla', Mujib declared unequivocally (167). Such political references from South Asia that align with the history of the region connect Ara's novel with the sociopolitical context of the 1971 war. The originality of the author's approach is called 'substantive contribution', a matrix of good ethnographic work as suggested by Richardson (2000).

Women are supposed to play traditional roles and restrict their way of life; otherwise, they are blamed by society (Wakelin and Long 2003, 477). Patriarchy thinks that women are the weaker sex and are, therefore, incapable of performing tough tasks like being male soldiers in male-regulated regimes (Snow 1994, 382). In *Blame*, most of the women are shown to be passive, submissive to the male authority and oblivious to politics and national affairs (Ara 2015, 217). Even participating in political processions and shouting slogans with the men is considered inappropriate. However, there are also women like Laila in *Blame*, who emerge as courageous women. She comes to Dhaka for higher education, freeing herself from the restrictions of patriarchy and the tag of being a Kazi girl. Her infatuation with Santo reflects her solid mettle as a 'love affair between any Hindu boy and Muslim girl was bound to have devastating consequences' (154). Her decision to participate in politics, to be an activist and, finally, to be a freedom fighter are all highly criticised with her being blamed several times by her mother, her brother and the rest of society. In a community where women are born and brought up to be faithful homemakers, devoted daughters and loyal wives, Laila's attempt to break with tradition brings much condemnation for her. 'This might make you into an unmarriageable girl', her mother often tells her (203).

People blame those who have experienced sexual assault, arguing that their attitudes, their manners and the way they dressed provoked the perpetrators to act violently towards them and that the victims themselves enjoyed the event to an extent (Wakelin and Long 2003, 477). Laila's involvement in politics, her dress code, her hairstyle and her carrying a gun like a male soldier break the traditional notion of womanhood, and she is blamed by all in society except for a few characters such as Santo, Kamil and Alam Khan. Ara, too, defends Laila's courageous attitude. She, through Laila, takes a completely anti-sexist attitude to war and asserts, 'War and death don't care about gender' (2015, 233). Through her portrayal of Laila, Ara questions why a woman cannot play the role of a warrior when she can be a victim of war (234). Accordingly, Laila declares that as a native of Bangladesh, the war of liberation is her war too. Overcoming all hurdles, Laila takes up a gun to free her nation from the bloodthirsty Pakistani regime, defying the conventional image of 'a sari-clad Bengali girl' (241). She is not afraid of death because she knows that in war, people do not chase death but that death chases them. She is no longer afraid of what society thinks of her because by participating in the war to free her nation, she has found her agency and inner calling. Ara writes:

> She knew they would never forgive her and, if things got worse, they might even disown her. Regardless of whether her decision had been right, Laila was proud of herself that she had made it. It was her decision. She was no longer a child—now she owned herself. For the first time in her life she experienced how it felt to follow one's inner call. (242)

On a similar note, Yasmin Saikia also expresses her sorrow over the institutional silence of the country on women's issues and affirms that survivors can speak if they are allowed to do so (2004, 277). Laila does not lose her spirit and voice even after being raped, humiliated and blamed by society. She declares, 'I will go and fight for Gita, and die if necessary. A death like that would be a thousand times more honourable than living my life as a tarnished woman' (Ara 2015, 298). Laila raises her voice against the sexist definition of war heroes in society. She blames society for only glorifying men for their heroic deeds in war, whereas women are reviled and reprimanded for the same heroic deeds.

Women have often been targeted in war-torn areas for rape and sexual violence and displaced from their homes. A rape victim is blamed for her victimisation if she does not follow her gender role in society (Wakelin and Long 2003, 477). The epilogue of the novel shows the plight of the Birangona in Bangladesh. The independent nation state has silenced the voices of the Birangona in various ways. Their rehabilitation after the war by the then Bangladesh government was an initial step meant to glorify the women who sacrificed their chastity for the formation of the nation (Murshed 1997, 120). Nayanika Mookherjee interrogates the level of public secrecy regarding the lives of the Birangona, who are worshipped in Bangladeshi popular culture as brave and courageous women but are ultimately blamed in society through continual *khota* or sarcastic remarks (2006, 434–435). In Bangladesh, women think that it is better to die than to live with their experience of *shorom* (shame)—a condition which has been compared with that of the mythological character Sita who asked Mother Earth to split and swallow her to save her from her disgrace (Mookherjee 2015b, 58). A famous photograph by Naibuddin Ahmed shows that the condition of the Birangona in postcolonial Bangladesh is horrible and contradictory to the image of brave heroines that the word conjures. In this photograph, a Birangona is shown with dishevelled hair and a covered face, indicating her attempt to escape the shame and blame of being raped (Mookherjee 2015a, 381). Ahmed's photograph is one of the visual representations of the rape survivors of the 1971 war that captured much public and artistic attention during the war as well as in the contemporary time. When the photograph was first published in the *Washington Post*, it damaged the image of the Pakistani forces who were continuously defending their position to the global community to maintain normalcy (*Daily Star* 2008). When Tahmima Anam visited a photographic exhibition at Rivington Place, a public gallery in East London, she was inspired by the power of Ahmed's visual representation to tell the stories of the 1971 war. In an article in the *Guardian*, Anam says, 'This is just one of many haunting images that make up Bangladesh 1971' (2008). Ahmed's photograph powerfully appeals to global readers and critics to comprehend the level of gender violence in the 1971 war and the public secrecy associated with it. The description of the photograph comprises a major portion of Nayanika Mookherjee's narratives of the rape survivors in her article (2015a) and book (2015b). She shows how the post-war consciousness of Bangladeshi people about the rape survivors is largely connected to the portrayal of a victim in Ahmed's photograph. Mookherjee begins the preface of her book with a description of Ahmed's photograph and its exposure at the domestic and international levels (2015b). She asserts that 'Ahmed's photograph is iconic, symbolizing the horrors of 1971 and connoting the supposed shame and anonymity of the raped woman' (xv). Thereafter, the image has been reproduced in different ways in books, exhibitions and theatres to tell the readers and the audience the plights of the Birangona in Bangladesh. In the exhibition titled 'Bangladesh 1971' at Rivington Place Gallery in Shoreditch, East London, Naibuddin Ahmed's hair photograph (titled 'One of the estimated 400,000 birangona meaning "brave women", who were raped during the war') appeared to be the 'visual trace of the raped women' (Mookherjee 2015a, 382; 2015b, xvi). This hair photograph, along with several other visual and literary representations, gives an impression that the society and the family of these war heroines have deserted them (Mookherjee 2015b, xix). However, there are other narratives too. Mookherjee describes many instances in which raped women were supported, accepted and recognised in contemporary Bangladesh (2015b). We will cover these narratives more extensively in Chapter 4 and Chapter 5.

The position of rape survivors in contemporary Bangladeshi society and the level of public secrecy are some of the main concerns in Ara's novel *Blame*. This novel shows both the prevailing conditions: the denial of raped women's position in the postcolonial society of Bangladesh and their acceptance in the same society when they fight back. When Jamil inquires as to the whereabouts of Laila to Mullah

Yousef, the latter advises Jamil, 'A disgraced woman is better left alone. Still better forgotten' (Ara 2015, 281). Ara further illustrates the issue through Laila's mother's response to her situation:

> Hasna Begum had not spoken a word about Laila since she had been abducted; it was as though she didn't know who Laila was, as though she had never had a daughter called Laila. Hasna Begum's lips were shut, she showed neither grief nor anxiety—for who would wish to bear the burden of disgrace brought to a family by a daughter imprisoned at a military camp? (272–273)

Such indifference and silence overshadow the life of Laila and many like her who were abducted and sexually assaulted by the Pakistani military. They face alienation from not only society but also their family members. Their abduction is a one-way journey. In a certain sense, they were compelled to leave their home, never to return. Even when they returned physically, their presence went unacknowledged.

In the case of social blaming, a warrant is an integral part, and the blamer is persuaded to show reasonable grounds why the agent is to blame (Malle et al. 2014, 149). People are busy with the blame game in Ara's novel, without justifying the blame they assign. The blamers in the novel are preoccupied with social taboos (rape being one) and religious orthodoxy. A raped woman is blamed for her victimisation just on the assumption that society would not approve of her even though the woman had no hand in her victimisation. Rape survivors are supposed to receive justice and support, but in reality, they are blamed by all, sometimes even by other survivors (Wakelin and Long 2003, 477). Though Gita receives support from her family after her return from the Pakistani army camp, she is blamed by society first for being abducted by the Pakistani army and then for being a lower-class Hindu girl abducted by Muslim men. Thinking of her prospects in society, Jamil is afraid to rescue her from the camp as this society would blame her for bringing disgrace and for being a 'fallen woman' (Ara 2015, 321). Despite being sympathetic towards Gita, her family disowns her in fear and never comes back to look after her (334). The blame game continues even between Laila and Gita, who had been the closest of friends since childhood. Gita blames Laila for being disowned by her family and for her status in society as a 'disgraceful whore' (335).

The women who survived sexual violence in the 1971 genocide were blamed by society and disowned by their families for carrying war babies (D'Costa 2011, 195). Bina D'Costa's interview with Dr Geoffrey Davis, a medical graduate from Sydney, New South Wales, underlines the role of blame in wiping out thousands of raped Bengali women in post-liberation Bangladesh. Dr Davis was appointed as a medical officer in Bangladesh for six months in 1972 by international organisations such as United Nations Population Fund (UNFPA) and World Health Organization (WHO) to oversee the process of abortion or adoption of war babies. In the interview with D'Costa, he said that many women wished to keep their babies alive, but unfortunately, they were forced to kill them to get rid of the blame for polluting society. In *Blame*, Laila and Gita are considered defiled because they have been raped. However, unlike some other Bengali women, Ara's protagonists are courageous enough to stand up to the very society that defiled them and refers to them as 'polluted'. When Laila and Gita walk towards the rehabilitation centre, everyone closes their doors because witnessing raped women and women pregnant with war babies is a matter of disgrace to them (Ara 2015, 366). They know that they have been living in a society devoid of justice. Women are born here only to be blamed. They still hold on to the courage to go on with their lives: 'To them it was just the last station on a long journey. There was no going back. They had come far; the journey from now would be on a different route' (366).

The postcolonial crisis of identity in Ara's novel is prominent, with the war being solely blamed for the crisis the nation faced during the time. Ara shows war as a multifaceted game with many other functions apart from killing people, raping women and demolishing properties.

When people become refugees and struggle for freedom in their native land, it becomes a crucial face of war (Ara 2015, 186). When Laila watches Aunt Sima naked in her madness, she is reminded of another face of war, 'a naked face' (191). While travelling in a boat overnight to find a safe shelter during the war, Laila explores another face of war, one 'smeared with sweat, urine and excrement' (220). War and blame both appear to be games to the people who engage in war actively or passively. When Gita is captured by the Pakistani army, she is not only raped and humiliated but also becomes an object of the war game as well as the blame game. One of the soldiers proposes to another soldier in the camp in which Gita is imprisoned: 'We each pull a card. If we pull a red card in succession, we will kill this infidel.... And if the cards are mixed colours? ... Then we throw her out into the yard' (318).

Emphasising the positive aspect of social blame, Malle, Guglielmo and Monroe suggest that 'blame emerges as one of the most accepted forms of moral criticism, along with finding fault and pointing the finger. The acts that are least socially acceptable and most unlike blame are attacking, slandering, and vilifying' (2014, 171). Ara faithfully captures the sentiment of social blame that engulfs the sociopolitical landscape of the Liberation War. In most cases, blame is devoid of any morality for her because it has been exploited to victimise the Bengali civilians, demolish resources, torment Biharis and rape Bengali women. While attributing social blame, emotions have to be fully controlled for an unbiased outcome (Malle et al. 2014, 171). The author has multiple emotions connected with the birth of Bangladesh, but unlike South Asian historians and novelists, she successfully puts aside her personal feelings to provide her version of the truth. Ara's characters being the agents of blame is supported by contemporary ethnographic research conducted in the country that shows that women were ostracised by their families (D'Costa 2011; Ibrahim 2017). They were thought of as inauspicious (Saikia 2011b). As a feminist ethnographic novel, Ara's novel expresses reality, a parameter of good ethnographic work (Richardson 2000). Where most Bangladeshi narratives are unidimensional, representing the Pakistanis as perpetrators of violence, Bengali nationalists as war heroes and Bengali women as victims of rape, Ara's novel showcases the bitter side of the war, especially through the portrayal of the victimisation of non-Bengali people in an independent Bangladesh. Therefore, blame appears to be a pretext for Pakistan and Bangladesh to try to nullify their crimes during the Bangladesh Liberation War.

Women's Agency in Tahmima Anam's *A Golden Age*

Women constitute an essential half of society, which is true even during wartime. Though history has projected war as a men's affair, women participate actively, sometimes even as armed fighters (Karam 2000, 2). Contemporary postcolonial feminist writers and critics debate over the representation of women as marginalised, subjugated and victimised in a patriarchal society. In the South Asian context, women's negligible position in history and disregard for their agency in the conflicts are due to the focus being mainly on their victimisation and subjugation. The reason behind this is the influence of Western projection and Western sponsorship of the academic endeavours of the Global South. Hence, sexual violence in war, especially in the conflicts of the Global South, has become a familiar topic in academia. According to Swati Parashar, feminist scholars in the Global South more or less select their case studies based on the funding schemes of Western governments and themes selected by them. She writes: 'Case studies are carefully selected to suit the Western governments' strategic priorities, intervention goals, and funding rationale; some areas are over-researched (like sexual violence in wars), while others are marginalized (such as state violence against indigenous people and gender minorities' (Parashar 2018, 6). Parashar's remark on the representation also tallies with Gayatri Chakraborty Spivak's debate on the term *subaltern*, which is generally applied to the women of South Asian regions to show that they are a marginalised and deprived section of society. Spivak (in an interview with Leon de Cock) warned us against the excessive use of the word *subaltern*, which has become a 'classy' word to represent the oppressed according to her. Instead, she suggests that *subaltern* is a term broadly associated with someone's powerlessness to access the cultural sphere (Cock 1992, 45). As women have their multiple stories of struggle, survival and courageous deeds, homogenising women in South Asian regions through the lens of Western feminists deprives them of their historical and political agency (Mohanty 2003, 39).

South Asian historiography, particularly the official history of Bangladesh, has focused only on the subaltern position of women and has avoided the positive agency of women in nation-making. The Bangladesh government's official publication, *Bangladesher Shadhinota Juddha: Dolilpotro*, hardly mentions the role of women in the war (Rahman [1982] 2009). In a few places, women are mentioned along with children as victims and are counted as numbers without any proper attribution (quoted in Rahman [1982] 2009, 184–188). Srinath Raghavan's *1971: A Global History of the Creation of Bangladesh* is another work in global academia that documents the history of the 1971 war. However, it avoids the intensity of gendered violence and the positive agency of women in the war. Instead, Raghavan emphasises the controversy about the number of victims and suggests that the figures are speculative (2013, 12). The denial of history regarding the agency of women does not prove that women were merely victims in the war. Recent media portrayals and intervention in feminist ethnographic fiction and non-fiction have unearthed plenty of instances where women worked side by side with men as activists, fighters, nurses, policy makers and more during the war and in its aftermath. Taramon Bibi, who fought in the war and was awarded the title 'Bir Pratik'[1] by the Bangladeshi government in 1995, received media coverage recently (Amin et al. 2016). Despite the prolonged neglect in history, feminist thinkers and writers in Bangladesh and throughout South

Asian regions have focused on women's agency in the war, denying that their only role was that of victims. The representation of valiant women features in the literature and the visual culture of Bangladesh since the 1971 war. Noted historian Willem van Schendel has pointed out instances of such valiant Bengali women during the freedom struggle of Bangladesh with illustrations from many Bangladeshi literary narratives (2009, 165).

Bangladeshi writing in English has intervened in various types of war narratives in the last two decades. Fictional narratives by Bangladeshi writers such as Dilruba Z. Ara, Tahmima Anam, Ruby Zaman and others are different from the earlier war narratives of Bangladesh mainly because of two reasons: women's agency has been broadly focused on, and women's experiences in the war have not been homogenised. One such novel is Ruby Zaman's *Invisible Line* (2011), which shows the survival of a woman born to a Bihari father and a Bengali mother. The novel shows the multifaceted roles played by women from Bihari, Bengali and Pakistani communities and whose lives had been greatly affected due to the formation of the new nation state of Bangladesh (Mohua and Mowtushi 2019, 540). Swedish-Bangladeshi novelist Dilruba Z. Ara's novel *Blame* is another fictional work that shows Bangladeshi women's power of resistance and their active participation as armed fighters during the 1971 war (2015). Tahmima Anam's *A Golden Age* is also a courageous tale of women's agency in the 1971 war. Women in her novel are portrayed less as victims and more as caregivers, diplomats, social workers and fighters (2007).

Rehana Haque, the female protagonist of Anam's *A Golden Age*, is a secular, spirited woman in Bangladesh, a country that seems to be dominated by Islamic orthodox ideology during and after the 1971 war. Women in 1960s East Pakistan and 1970s Bangladesh are often portrayed in history and fiction as raped, marginalised and silenced in a war-torn country. This representation might be a projection of the academia of the Global North, and the historians and writers of the Global South conform to such Western projections (Parashar 2018, 6). Schendel writes of many positive instances of the agency of Bengali women in Bangladesh in the 1960s and the 1970s (2009). He shows that women in Bangladesh were the bearers of rich Bengali cultural heritage at that time and lived a liberal and choice-based life (2009, 34). Not only that, women living in urban and city areas were also highly politically conscious and participated in political movements before the 1971 war. Anam's representation of Rehana Haque agrees with Schendel's representation of liberal women during the Liberation War. Due to Rehana Haque's secular outlook, she has Hindu tenants and is passionately moved by their distress after Operation Searchlight on 25 March 1971 when Hindus were made special targets. This outlook does not mean that she hates religion. She offers namaz but is never orthodox (Anam 2007, 162). She is comfortable taking her children to watch a cricket match in the stadium and equally comfortable taking them to watch *Cleopatra*. All these happened during the critical phase when the judge in Rehana's trial (for the legal custody of her children after her husband's death) disapproves of the matter, referring to the film as unsuitable for the children (6). Anam's voice seems critical when Rehana is not admitted to the graveyard where her husband is buried just because she is a woman (19). She chooses to side with Bangladesh because of her love for the deprived nation.

Women in Third World countries, especially in the war-afflicted regions of Asia and Africa, are supposedly not politically conscious. Throughout the history of feminist writings, Western academia and its counterpart in the East have projected a homogenous image of Asian women, and their stories are mainly based on their subordination in society. However, this type of representation is affected by the politics of representation because thinking of women of different countries as members of the single group 'women' compels us to study the group based on a general notion of their subordination (Mohanty 1984, 344). In *A Golden Age*,

Anam portrays women in urban and city areas of East Pakistan as highly politically conscious, playing important roles in the war and policy making, though mostly indirectly (2007). Though Rehana's ethnicity is that of Urdu-speaking Pakistanis and most of her family members live in Pakistani metropolises like Lahore and Karachi, Rehana chooses to side with Bangladesh. Rehana is very eager to fight for the justice that struggling East Pakistan deserved. When the war of 1971 breaks out, 'she discovers that, for all her inability to "replace her mixed tongue with a pure Bengali one", it is the East that is now "home"; it is Bangladesh for which she will make the greatest sacrifices' (Burton-Hill 2007). Whenever she goes to visit her husband's grave before the genocide, she promises her husband her loyalty to the nation. She tells her husband that she and her children are waiting for Mujib to win the next election and come to power. She is hopeful that, under Mujib's leadership, the country will see new days, and her children will be able to start their studies again (Anam 2007, 20). The youngsters of the country, like her son Sohail, become restless after Mujib wins the Pakistani general election in 1970 and expect some drastic action from him. Rehana, like a wise diplomat, assures them, 'Mujib is a canny politician … he must know something we don't' (28). Under Rehana's liberal parenthood, Sohail becomes a liberal thinker and an uncompromising voice. He cannot control his outbursts about the discrimination East Pakistan continuously faces from the West Pakistani rulers: 'West Pakistan is bleeding us out. We earn most of the foreign exchange. We grow the rice, we make the jute, and yet we get nothing—no schools, no hospitals, no army. We can't even speak our own bloody language!' (29). Sohail is against any type of compromise with the West Pakistani rulers. He suggests that Mujib should declare independence instead (29). Unlike her friends Mrs Rahaman and Mrs Chowdhury, Rehana never blames Sohail for his association with contemporary politics. She blames the unethical rule and enforced discrimination of West Pakistan for everything.

She remembers how her son's involvement with politics began. The problem started after 1948 when the Pakistani government started to impose Urdu in a Bengali-majority land. They took away the revenue of huge jute production and established factories not in Dhaka but in Islamabad and Karachi (33).

Tahmima Anam's character Rehana Haque is a completely unconventional war heroine who is free from the obligation of merely being a victim in the war (Biswas and Tripathi 2017, 527). Rehana's image in Anam's *A Golden Age* can be summed up in two categories: first, as the mother of Sohail and Maya and, second, as a brave fighter in the freedom struggle of Bangladesh. After her husband's death, when Rehana's son and daughter are taken away to Lahore by her brother-in-law, she fights legal battles alone to get custody of her children. She loses everything, starting from her husband's Vauxhall to her jewellery, but she never regrets it (Anam 2007, 35–36). When she wants to construct an apartment on her vacant land, she tries for a loan, but she faces physical harassment from the bank manager (36). After fighting for the legal custody of her children, when she gets them, the time comes to bid them farewell. When Sohail joins the guerrilla regiment and makes their house *Shona*[2] the den of the guerrilla fighters, Rehana could not be angry. She is proud because she has taught her son how to take charge in a serious situation (101–102). Rehana and Maya together represent the preservers of *Bangaliyana*,[3] when Bengali rituals, Bengali songs and celebrations of Bengali festivals were banned in Bangladesh. Her love for Bengali nationalism inspires her to move from singing ghazals to singing the banned Bengali songs (76). What makes Rehana unique is her strong mind to study the faces of others and gauge their intentions and her strong control over her emotions in hard times. When she listens to her beloved son Sohail's description of life in a battle camp as a guerrilla fighter, of staying in a tent without home comfort and eating on banana leaves, she suppresses her emotions so that Sohail does not become weak (100). She pretends to be strong in front of her son just to deliver the message that saving the country is a sacred mission and that one cannot think of personal comfort and happiness.

Rehana's motherhood in the novel is more than biological. She emerges as the universal mother to every member of the Muktibahini who struggled for the nation (Biswas and Tripathi 2017, 528). Women's agency in the war is manifold, from being fighters to caregivers. Rehana's support, care and participation transform her into the mother of a nation, not only Sohail and Maya (Anam 2007, 111). She does not like Sabeer initially when Sabeer marries her son's beloved. However, she then rescues Sabeer, risking her own life, and prays to God for Sabeer's physical pain and mental trauma from prolonged torture in the Pakistani camp to end (201). Due to her obligation to the nation, she could not pardon her brother-in-law Faiz who was once a Pakistani collaborator and a mastermind during the genocide. She could have spared him, but the image of Joy, Aref and other dead soldiers and the silent face of Mrs Sengupta appear before her, leaving her no choice (272–273). The universality in Rehana's character is what makes her the most unique heroine in Bangladeshi writings in English. She represents the secular spirit of Bangladesh, the same spirit that helped the people of East Pakistan form a nation based on their ethnicity in defiance of the Partition and Two Nations Theory based on religion. Unlike other war narratives of Bangladesh that show women mostly as passive observers of the war, Anam's narrative shows that women can be fighters, volunteers, policy makers and even diplomats. In March 1971, when there is a curfew outside and homeless people jostle around Rehana's garden, she feeds them with whatever resources she has (62). The same Rehana moves to the refugee camps in Kolkata and does more inspiring tasks, such as talking to the refugees stranded there to keep them motivated during hard times (223). In the refugee camp, she helps Dr Rao in his visits, taking records of the medicines and writing the prescriptions (229). She befriends the people in the camps and the hospitals, and they call her *apa* (elder sister) (231). When Sohail and his friends use her house to store arms and rations for the fighters and refugees, Rehana tactfully keeps her friends away (103). After sending her daughter to the refugee camp in Kolkata and her son to fight in the freedom movement, she lies to her neighbours that she has sent them to Karachi to her relatives' home (130). When Sabeer is caught by the Pakistani army, Sohail approaches his mother for his rescue because he knew that his mother could convince his uncle Faiz in this regard and she could trick the Pakistani army with her fluent Urdu (168). To rescue Sabeer, she moves from one thana to another in the darkness. She bribes a police officer even when her security is at stake (193–201). She plays a trick on a Pakistani colonel and saves her daughter with her Urdu-speaking skills, which makes the Pakistanis think that she too is Pakistani (259–265).

Tahmima Anam's writing technique resembles that of naturalistic writers[4] who showed that literature should not strive to find morality or poetic justice because life is not like that in reality. The 'stunning' debut novel, the first fiction in Anam's trilogy, not only talks about war, brutality, inhumanity and prejudices against the refugees but also food, song and, most importantly, love (Burton-Hill 2007). The protagonist of this novel is no exception when it comes to the question of human passion and lovemaking. The major brought to Rehana's life feelings of love that she had never realised existed. 'She hadn't been all alone. She'd watched *Mughal-e-Azam* and fallen in love with a stranger and uttered words she'd kept hidden for more than a decade' (Anam 2007, 224). Love appears to her in a very troublesome moment of war, and she responds to it wholeheartedly, though she suffers due to a moral obligation to her dead husband. She breaks the decorum of the age in many ways: she performs prayers with unrelated males like the major, and she leads the prayer (112). She reveals her feelings and all her unsaid words to the major. She tells him the secrets of her past life and about her son's love affair with the neighbouring girl who became a victim of religious orthodoxy, the dirty flat in Dhaka where her son now lives a secret life and so much more (167–168). When the war is about to end with a treaty, Rehana asks forgiveness from her husband

and God, for she could not control her human passions of love and affection. It seems to her that she has betrayed her husband and God (274). Women are blamed if they do not follow their traditional roles in society and restrict their way of life (Wakelin and Long 2003, 477). Rehana is blamed on several occasions for her children's decision to join the war as fighters and activists. As she is a single woman in a patriarchal society, the blame is always directed at her even when she is not responsible. When her brother-in-law Faiz learns that Rehana's daughter Maya has become an activist, he accuses Rehana of ruining his brother's son and daughter (Anam 2007, 189). However, unlike most other women under a patriarchal regime, Rehana is not just a subject to be blamed. She defends herself by allowing her son and daughter to participate in the war. She questions the loyalty of Pakistani collaborators like Faiz when women like Sharmeen are raped, tortured and killed (191).

In Anam's novel, Maya is the second most important female figure who exemplifies women's agency in the war. Maya also shows a trace of her mother's humane spirit. During the cyclone of 1970, when many dead bodies are washed away and the government is surprisingly silent about the calamity, Sohail and Maya join the rescue camp and do their best to save people. Maya joins the students' Communist Party and donates all her clothes to the victims, remaining clad in only a white saree (Anam 2007, 33–34). She works as a typist and helps her brother Sohail and his allies to issue press releases from the hideaway in *Shona*, the house which has turned into the headquarters of the guerrilla movement of freedom fighters (102). After the victimisation of Sharmeen, one of Maya's closest friends, Maya devotes her life to the freedom struggle. She migrates to Kolkata to help the Bengali refugees there in several camps such as the Salt Lake refugee camps. Due to her mother's influence, Maya learns to sing ghazals, but her political life leads her to practise the banned songs of Tagore[5] more than the ghazals (76). When the civil war erupts in the whole country, Maya leads the students at the University of Dhaka, and she is very eager to contribute directly to the freedom struggle of Bengalis (87–88). Like Rehana, Maya lives a choice-based life, which is why she is thrilled by Rabindranath Tagore's *Gitanjali* at a time when it is banned in East Pakistan (255). When Maya's friend Sharmeen goes missing, when East Pakistan is at the peak of civil war and when millions of people become refugees in the border area of India, Maya joins the movement, putting aside all obligations. Maya says, 'I can't sit back and do nothing, Ma. Everyone is fighting. Even people who weren't sure, people who wanted to stay with Pakistan' (79–80). Rehana has no choice except to control her motherly feelings for her son and daughter when they want to go for the sacred duty of saving the nation. When Sohail and Maya leave, Rehana never lets herself feel lonely. She spends her days counting the resources preserved in her house for freedom fighters and exploring the level of violence wrought upon the whole country (85).

Tahmima Anam's novel shows that women's roles and plights in the context of the 1971 war in Bangladesh can hardly be generalised according to their ethnicity. Ethnically, Rehana belongs to the Urdu-speaking community that has a connection with Pakistan. Despite that, Anam's protagonist Rehana Haque is greatly attached to the Bengali language and culture. Even her Bengali pronunciation is purer than her Urdu pronunciation; she is occasionally scolded by her sister Marzia about it as she is betraying the community of Urdu-speaking people (Anam 2007, 18). Maya experiences bullying in her school where she is tagged as 'Bihari' just because she has relatives in Lahore (45). When the war begins in East Pakistan, Rehana's sisters escape to Karachi. Her brother-in-law, too, supports Pakistan, and they believe in the ideology of a united Pakistan. During and after the 1971 war, Urdu-speaking Bihari people in East Pakistan were considered the enemies of the Bengali community because they shared an ethnic connection with the Pakistanis, and sometimes, they were accused of collaborating in mass rape and genocides (Ibrahim 2017, 117). In this novel, Urdu-speaking butchers are tagged as collaborators with the Pakistani army (Anam 2007, 118–119). Anam's protagonist stays apart from such generalisation. Despite having an ethnic connection with Urdu-speaking Pakistanis, Rehana, like a sensible human being, opposes their crimes against humanity. When most of her relatives migrate to Pakistan, she never thinks of moving to Pakistan to live with the oppressors of the Bengalis (86). At the end of the novel, the feelings expressed by Rehana to her dead husband in a letter reveal how much she loves Bangladesh and how she cherishes her dream of a new country that was about to be born.

> The war will end today.... There will be a pressing crowd on the pavement but Maya will elbow us to the front. A boy will sell flags for two taka and everyone will wave and crane their necks to see the road. Coloured paper will sail from buildings; fists will wave in the air; there will be dancing, a man on a flute, a woman beating a *dhol* slung across her shoulder ... we are spellbound, lovebound, home-bound, singing '*How I love you, my golden Bengal*.' The sky is pale and iridescent and today the war has ended, and today I will clutch my flag, hold my breath and wait for our son. (Anam 2007, 274)

Rehana's attachment to her home, *Shona*; the land where she lives; the people with whom she engages and people's feelings for the land cause her to love Bangladesh (though the name 'Bangladesh' was yet to come). These touching words of Rehana reveal that her feelings and efforts for newborn Bangladesh would be very hard to measure from the perspective of the ethnic politics associated with the 1971 war. Indira Gandhi, the first woman prime minister of India, is a great example of women's agency in the context of the Liberation War of Bangladesh. When the war began, Indira Gandhi offered all possible help, sheltered millions of refugees and established training camps in West Bengal, Tripura, Assam, Meghalaya and Bihar to train the Bengali freedom fighters (Andrio 2016, 737). When millions of refugees took shelter in the Indian state of West Bengal, Indira Gandhi pledged support for them and encouraged them with her belief that the free-spirited Bengalis would soon achieve their victory over the fascist government of Pakistan (Anam 2007, 98–99). In *A*

Golden Age, Rehana's contribution to the country as a shelter-giver and caregiver somewhat resembles Indira Gandhi's contribution to the nation. Like Indira Gandhi, Rehana shelters the freedom fighters, army personnel and civilians in the war, and like Indira Gandhi, she engages in diplomacy against Pakistan. Rehana, Maya and other freedom movement activists in the novel are highly ambitious about the Indo-Soviet treaties. They believe that if Indira Gandhi intervenes, they will win the war (212). Just like Indira Gandhi offered Bengalis arms, food and shelter and free access to India, Rehana gives Sohail permission to use their dream house, *Shona*, for all types of activities related to the freedom struggle.

Tahmima Anam's feminist ethnographic endeavour helped her to encompass the internal stories of women in Bangladesh during the 1971 war through the lens of a professional anthropologist. Her portrayal of women in *A Golden Age* is unconventional in the sense that other narratives of the war mainly focus on sexual violence, and Anam emphasises the positive agency of women in hard times instead. The representation of violence is internal rather than external—the violence of people against a single woman rather than the violence of the perpetrators against the women of an ethnic group. The novel shows the internal struggle of a woman against society, traditional beliefs and even family members to restore the rights of a single woman who lost everything in her battle. In Anam's novel, she projects that people who are not physically harmed in the war also suffered from mental injuries, and their trauma is no less than that of physical wounds. War kills people and brings atrocities to women, but many people are left physically unharmed. Anam's protagonists do not undergo any physical torture, but an important theme in this novel is the psychological trauma and the degradation of personal relationships against the backdrop of the war. The 1971 war caused the death of three million people and the rape of 200,000 to 400,000 women as per Bangladeshi narratives (Sundar and Sundar 2014, 44; Linton 2010b, 194). At the same time, it psychologically traumatised those who were left physically unharmed. Coping with the damaged civilisation and enduring the crisis of humanity are challenges for people like Rehana, the Senguptas and the other aristocrats in Dhaka, the largest city in East Pakistan (now Bangladesh). At the end of the novel, she confesses that the nine-month-long war seemed like it lasted nine generations. Her son had survived the war, but his friends died in the same war. Seeing so many burnt houses, demolished monuments and the suffering of humanity is traumatic (Anam 2007, 271).

Historians and researchers in the area of genocide and conflict studies often fail to recognise that 'women, and even children, have agency' in the war (Kaufman 2016, 1504). Tahmima Anam's novel narrates the incessant atrocities of the Pakistani army and two women's struggle to survive the whole situation. Rehana and Maya's courage goes beyond self-protection. They aim to help the victims and assist the freedom fighters to wage war against the Pakistanis and their Bengali collaborators. When history failed to record women's agency in the 1971 war, such fictional works, along with non-fictional narratives in newspapers and magazines, uncover instances of women's courage during the freedom struggle. Rape and extreme violence could not stop the female spirit of Bangladesh. Instead, women like Maya and Rehana thought that they needed to do something. With the characters of Rehana and Maya, Tahmima Anam has broken the tradition of male protagonists in the literature and popular culture on the Liberation War of Bangladesh. Rehana is the hero of the novel, and her deeds resemble the heroic deeds of many other Bengali women during the war. So, when Rehana reaches Kolkata to help her daughter in their service in the refugee camps, her daughter's friends say, 'You are an example to all of us. The hero!' (Anam 2007, 209). Apart from Rehana, Maya and her friends are also perfect specimens of the female spirit during the ethnic struggle. They show positive agency in the war by tending to wounded soldiers, driving trucks to transport rations for the refugees, writing pamphlets to inspire youngsters and so on (216, 218). Anam's representation of women's agency in the 1971 war exemplifies the actual roles played by women in Bangladesh during the war and its aftermath. Contemporary narratives of the war by anthropologists, human rights activists and media columnists have plenty of references to women's participation that go beyond their status as rape victims. As per the narratives of women recorded by Nayanika Mookherjee, women played significant roles to get justice for their victimisation in the trials of war criminals in Bangladesh almost five decades after the war (2006, 433–434). Women's subjugation due to the ethnic politics between the Bengali-speaking and the Urdu-speaking community is another issue raised by Anam in her fictional narrative, which was later rediscovered and reinvestigated by Sarmila Bose (2011a) and Yasmin Saikia (2011b). Later narratives by authors and anthropologists such as Bina D'Costa (2011), Yasmin Saikia (2011b) and Sarmila Bose (2011a) simply say that Tahmima Anam's ethnographic research on women's agency is undoubtedly a landmark to reinvestigate the agency of women in the 1971 war. Hence, her work is 'substantive' and a tool to 'express reality', two of Richardson's main matrixes of good ethnographical literature (2000). 'Reflexivity', a matrix to evaluate ethnography referring to the ethnographer's self-interest, subjectivity and self-exposure, is also present in her ethnographic intervention (Richardson 2000). Anam was raised in a family where most family members were associated with the war, and she interviewed several people in person before writing this novel. Women's experiences in the war in South Asian regions are critical for two reasons: first, to register their voice in their history, and second, to take them beyond their 'indigenous' and 'subaltern' position in Western narratives. Anam's women in her fictional representation of the 1971 war are not 'indigenous' or 'subaltern'. They are decision-makers, active fighters and diplomats. Such agency of women in the Liberation War will encourage the writers, researchers and activists of the age to reimagine the image of women in South Asia during/after the conflict.

Women's 'Cartographies of Struggle'

Chandra Talpade Mohanty implies that the traditional definition and the context of feminism, our endeavour to foreground certain contexts over others and the continuous shifts of the conceptual cartographies are all very important in the formation of the cartographies of the Third World women (2003, 45). Such context-specific or ethnically variable stories of women in the South Asian context have inspired fiction writing in the postcolonial era. Through the lens of feminist ethnography, ethnic conflicts evidently influence the lives of people, more specifically, women, even beyond geopolitical boundaries. In the 1971 war, women had to endure torture for ethnic struggles that were mainly between the men in the Pakistani military and Bengali Muktibahini. In the last two decades, the literature from Bangladesh and India has produced accounts of women who faced the war in Bangladesh. At the same time, very few works have portrayed the stories of Bengali women who migrated to Pakistan after the 1947 Partition for several reasons like livelihood and social stigmas. Kamila Shamsie, in her novel *Kartography*, portrays the lives of people in Karachi amidst the 1971 ethnic struggle between Bengalis and Pakistanis as well as the 1980s ethnic struggle between Pathans[6] and Muhajirs[7] (2002). The novel exemplifies how women become vulnerable targets in any ethnic conflict even if they do not have any direct involvement in it. Women, since the advent of civilisation, have played different roles in war, sometimes as armed fighters, sometimes as caregivers and sometimes also as victims. However, the gender-biased history evades the discussion of women's roles and contributions in any conflict. So, the researchers of the age have endeavoured to traverse through history to bring out the position, role and contribution of women in any ethnic conflict throughout the world (Kumar 2001, 68). Kamila Shamsie, a noted Pakistani writer and feminist activist, discusses women's engagement in ethnic conflicts in Pakistan and the level of solidarity women share with their ethnic group during the crucial time of conflict and in its aftermath.

Generally, ethnic conflicts are followed by migration because of the rise of post-conflict hatred and violence of the dominant ethnic group towards the dominated and vice versa. People migrated throughout South Asia after the 1947 Partition that divided nations based on religious and ethnic identity. Bengali-speaking Hindus migrated to West Bengal and Assam in India, Urdu-speaking Biharis migrated to Bangladesh, Urdu-speaking Muhajirs migrated to different areas of Pakistan and Punjabis switched their nations between India and Pakistan based on their religion. Many Bengalis migrated to Pakistan after the Partition for their livelihood because there was a huge demand for fisherfolk in the coastal areas of Pakistan (Mughal and Baloch 2017). Fictional narratives by Bangladeshi writers have hardly focused on the plight of Bengali women who lived outside Bangladesh and whose lives were indeed greatly affected by the ethnic struggle in the 1971 war. To address this narrative gap, Kamila Shamsie reframed the history of South Asia to connect women who were scattered in different nations as a consequence of ethnic struggle, remapping the 'cartography of struggle'[8] of the Third World women based on their race and ethnic identity. Mohanty, as a postcolonial feminist, has extensively discussed the necessity of cartography and its link to Third World women so that they do not yield to the theoretical praxis of Western feminism to determine their struggle. A pioneer of postcolonial feminism, Mohanty has always emphasised the necessity for women's intervention by South Asian researchers to determine the condition of the women of the region because she and other Third World feminists think that the Western projection of women of this region is quite political. She says: 'I see this as a map that will of necessity have to be redrawn as our analytic and conceptual skills and knowledge develop and transform the way we understand questions of history, consciousness, and agency' (2003, 45). Being a Pakistani writer with a lot of insight into the 1971 conflict between India, Bangladesh and Pakistan, Shamsie can rightfully create a postcolonial feminist approach towards highlighting the deplorable condition of South Asian women as victims in the war and their agency in conflicts. Shamsie's approach to documenting the lives and struggles of women in *Kartography* can be exemplified as feminist ethnography because she has great consciousness of the demography and ethnic variations of Karachi and has sincerely studied the lives of the people (in this case, Bengali people, in general, and Bengali women, in particular) in this city. Feminist ethnography as a methodology focuses on the research on communities of women. 'Feminist ethnography could focus on women's relationship to other women and the power differentials between them' (Visweswaran 1994, 20).

The Bengali ethnic group shares a deep-rooted history with the Pakistani cosmopolitan city of Karachi, and the city's connection with Bengalis dates back to the 1947 Partition. The migration of the Bengali community started in 1947 after the Partition when Pakistan was divided into two wings scattered on two sides of India. After the Partition, East Pakistan, which later became Bangladesh after a bloody revolution in 1971, faced social and economic subjugation from West Pakistan, which housed the central government of Pakistan. East Pakistan had a rich cultural heritage and was one of the highest jute-producing regions in the world. Despite contributing a major part of the revenue, East Pakistan got a minimum allotment from the union budget for education, security and healthcare. The prolonged discrimination became one of the reasons for the mass migration of the people of East Pakistan to its western wing, where they started to find better employment opportunities. Withdrawal of A category visas, no prospect of industrialisation and the pressure of an over-bounded economy in India were the reasons why the Bengali community was forced to migrate to Pakistan, denying their cultural tradition (Lambert 1959, 51).

As Karachi became the hub of Bengali migrants due to diverse work opportunities that suited them, Bengalis started to work in the fishing industry. Since their native lands were surrounded by many water bodies, fishing was a traditional occupation. *Machar Colony*, literally the fishermen's colony, in Karachi is a predominant Bengali community where Bengali people have continued to live for decades despite facing social prejudices, hatred and marginalisation at various levels. B.K. Mughal and S. Baloch write in their article 'The Woes of Bengalis, Burmese and Iranians of Karachi' that 75 per cent of the people of that colony of 85,000 residents are Bengali. The circumstances of women in that colony are pathetic for they come to the market area with their little children to work in a dirty atmosphere. The article focuses on the prevailing conditions:

> Uneven, dirt-filled streets wind along with tiny houses in Machar Colony. Heaps of rubbish are strewn everywhere. A horrible stench—the combination of moist sea wind, rotting fish, the sewage flowing through open drains and occasional smoke emitting from smouldering mounds of trash—engulfs the neighbourhood. (Mughal and Baloch 2017)

These women suffer as a marginalised class in filthy conditions, and without even a valid citizenship card, they have become vulnerable targets of trafficking. Trafficking of young Bengali women in metropolitan cities like Karachi for sexual slavery, forced marriage and sale is frequent (Gazdar 2003, 13). Shockingly, 200,000 Bengali women are reportedly trafficked in Pakistan at a rate of 200 to 400 women per month (25). Such references show that Bengalis live in Pakistan as second-class citizens, and women are vulnerable targets of sexual slavery there. This reference can be linked to Shamsie's representation of Bengali women in *Kartography*, in which she shows that having a Bengali mother or Bengali wife can bring Pakistanis hatred, shame and prejudice from fellow Pakistanis. The socially degraded Bengali women in Pakistan can be connected to the raped, degraded and dehumanised Bengali women in Bangladesh, and they forge solidarity based on their ethnic struggle in the 1971 war.

Apart from Bengali people, a large number of Urdu-speaking Bihari people also migrated from Bangladesh to Pakistan due to their ethnic connection. The non-Bengali Bihari people living in Bangladesh were accused of being connected to the Pakistani military during the civil war, and they migrated after the end of the war because they were being treated as enemies in Bangladesh (Gazdar 2003, 13). Other than migration for professional needs and due to social subjugation, migration also happened from Bangladesh to Pakistan to escape shame and hatred. Bina D'Costa, Yasmin Saikia and many contemporary writers have focused on the stigmatisation of women in Bangladesh after the end of the 1971 war because they were sexually assaulted by the Pakistani army and their Bengali collaborators. Many men killed their women in free Bangladesh because they had been raped during the war and, hence, were considered defiled, suggesting the inferior status of women in Bangladesh after the war (D'Costa 2011, 197–199). After independence, the rape survivors of the war were rehabilitated with education, shelter and job opportunities, and they were honoured with the title of 'Birangona' (the brave heroine of the war). Despite this, the Bangladeshi people were ashamed of the exposure of the story of a rape victim. Such negligence in the nation for which these women sacrificed a lot may have caused their migration to Pakistan. The migration of Bengali women to Pakistan with their rapists is one side of history that has also been neglected or bypassed in traditional historiographies. Newspaper articles and literary narratives have recently reinforced such issues in the history of South Asia. The migration of Bengali women with Pakistanis was probably first discussed in Neelima Ibrahim's *A War Heroine, I Speak* (2017). In this book, she writes of such instances where raped women migrated to Pakistan instead of living in free Bangladesh. They thought that living with their rapists would be easier than enduring hatred and blame from their dear ones (Ibrahim 2017, 64).

In Kamila Shamsie's *Kartography*, Maheen, a Bengali woman living in Pakistan, becomes a prospective target for abuse and humiliation. When and how Maheen came to Pakistan and the reasons for her association with Zafar and Ali remain a mystery. While living in Pakistan, Maheen shares a connection with the Bengali women in Bangladesh. Her mysterious lineage is unexplainable because, in Shamsie's words, '[m]any people can't even tell where she is from' (2002, 74). In the course of the narrative, readers learn that Maheen had been in Bangladesh after independence when Raheen's parents (Maheen's family friends) were getting married (36). Maheen is a Bengali woman who shares a strong bond with Bengali ethnicity even after living in Pakistan and creates a map based on ethnicity beyond the political line. She is regularly visited by her relatives from Bangladesh (41). She emerges as a marginalised Bengali woman living in Pakistan who suffers a lot but is not ready to yield to the system. Raheen loses Karim because Karim's mother, Maheen, is a Bengali, a member of the enemy class and one of the infidels trying to separate the nation in the eyes of Pakistanis. Karim is lost not for their deeds in the present; Karim was lost back in 1971 when Maheen started to feel an identity crisis after the independence of Bangladesh, much before Raheen and Karim were even born (277).

Being a woman in this world has political consequences, and women receive unjust treatment depending on their social and economic marginality (Mohanty 2003, 3). The sexual victimisation of a huge number of Bengali women happened in Bangladesh where women had a limited role in policy making. The Pakistani army raped thousands of Bengali women, and Pakistani people applauded such acts done to 'improve genes of the Bengalis' (Shamsie 2002, 189). After the civil war, Bengalis were treated as infidels, and they were sarcastically tagged 'Bingo'. Asif, a friend of Zafar, abuses a Bengali waiter in a restaurant in front of Maheen thus: 'Halfwit Bingo! Go back to your jungle' (183). Maheen, despite growing up in the aristocratic ambience of Karachi, feels humiliation at seeing such conduct, and she shows her empathy to that Bengali waiter. 'She was looking at the Bengali waiter. He walked past and caught her eye, and for a moment the barriers of class and gender became porous and something passed between them Zafar could not quite identify' (184). Maheen suddenly becomes an unwanted and troublesome figure in the aristocratic circles of Karachi after Pakistan is separated. Women have been considered passive and the subjects of subjugation due to their absence in policy making and the peace process. Their absence in the conflict prevention process is due to their non-participation in the State-centred system (Shoemaker 2002, 36). There are numerous cases in the recent war narratives where women played crucial roles through their direct involvement in the war. In many cases, women acted as a replacement for their men in the armed conflict. They became victims of war, sometimes killed, enslaved and viewed as property (Cook 2006, xxxii). The 1971 war influenced personal relationships, and women had to pay the ultimate cost. Though war broke everything, including the nation, in 1971, Maheen is hopeful that the bonding of love and affection will conquer ethnic hatred. She says to Zafar, 'War does crazy things to people, but wars end. I'll lie low, I promise that. And when it's over—please, God, soon!—we'll get married and have children and one day, every day, we'll tell them how we survived this inferno' (Shamsie 2002, 189). When Bangladesh became an independent nation, the Pakistani people could not tolerate that separation, and the Bengalis living in Pakistan became direct targets. Zafar sees the outburst of his neighbour and friend Shafiq because Bangladesh was free and he lost his brother in that ethnic struggle. Shafiq's words to Zafar show the intensity of his hatred towards Bengalis: 'Those bastards, those bastards, those Mukti Bahini bastards! They've won the war, let them have the country, let them have it. I never cared. Nor the way everyone else did' (230). Zafar is criticised because, unlike a typical Pakistani, he does not blame the Bengalis for their liberal spirit. Shafiq and other Pakistanis hate Zafar because he is going to marry a Bengali to let her have his children (231). After the 1971 war, people turn away from Maheen at parties, stop their conversations on seeing her and despise her to an extent (308). Zafar's condition is more deplorable. He is thought of as 'a turncoat, a traitor. A Bingo-lover' (308). Though born and raised in a Bengali family, Maheen has spent a major part of her life in the cosmopolitan ambience of Karachi. Suddenly, after the 1971 war, she faces marginalisation in several ways as she is considered a foreigner in her familiar Karachi (309).

Rape is used as an act of power for 'subjecting the enemy, disrupting familial traditions, and inflicting shame on the vanquished—females but also males, who were powerless to protect their women' (Cook 2006, xxxi). In the case of the 1971 war, rape was a vital weapon to demoralise the spirit of Bengali nationalism. The intensity and brutality of rape were so extreme that many women, whether they were eight or seventy-five, were raped up to eighty times a day (Gakhar 2018). Though the stories of rape and victimisation in the 1971 war got a place in many South Asian narratives, very few narratives portrayed women's experiences in the same war in a different context. Hence, a 're-story' is important because women's stories are often embedded with the gendered stories of society (Lee 1997, 2).

In *Kartography*, though women's direct victimisation by the military is referred to in very few places, it is marital rape that is intended as a weapon to degrade a community. Zafar's intention to marry a Bengali woman is not on any humanitarian grounds, nor is it because of affection. His justification tells us that the decision is politically motivated. He says, 'How can I marry one of them? Can I let one of them bear my children? Think of it as a civic duty. I'll be diluting her Bengali bloodline' (Shamsie 2002, 232). His intention to pollute the Bengali bloodline is the political purpose of rape that happens during wartime by the army. His civic duty refers to his duty towards Pakistan, that is, to take revenge on the Bengalis. A woman is supposed to be the perfect medium for taking such revenge because, through her, a Pakistani like Zafar would be able to transmit Pakistani blood into a Bengali womb, making the whole community feel degraded. Zafar's motive for marrying Maheen can be theorised as marital rape. In marital rape, class, ethnicity, race, gender and the like play vital roles to determine who can rape and who can be raped (Yllö and Torres 2016, 13).

Maheen's Bengali identity creates one type of identity crisis for her in Pakistan. Not only that, her son Karim's life is full of ambiguity for being 'half-Bengali' (Shamsie 2002, 42). Her Bengali nationality is also responsible in many ways for Maheen's break-up with Zafar. Zafar's suffering for having a Bengali fiancée is apparent in many places in the narrative. 'Bengali' became synonymous with 'infidel'. Even for having a Bengali fiancée, Zafar has to listen to comments like 'Our clients won't like working with someone who has a Bengali wife' (52). Maheen loses Zafar because he could not endure the hatred for being the husband of a Bengali, a 'Bingo'. Zafar ends his relationship with Maheen because it was easier for him to love a woman who was not a Bengali (300). Maheen struggles in her relationship with Zafar and even in her relationship with her husband Ali. When she divorces Ali, she had to shoulder the blame. Aunty Runty, a friend of Raheen's parents and Karim's parents, blames Maheen: 'Maheen, an adulteress! Has she no consideration for her son?' (122). Maheen belongs to the aristocratic class in the Karachi metropolis, but her social status did not protect her from being abused. Women become palpable targets of the patriarchal society, and their education, social class or aristocracy hardly protects them from physical and sexual abuse (Ptacek 2016, 125). Maheen formed a sisterhood with the other Bengali women in Bangladesh while mapping the cartography based on their struggle.

Conclusion

In most cases, ethnographic works are non-fictional because they are meant to portray real events rather than imaginary narratives. However, recent works by ethnographers and anthropologists suggest that ethnography can be fictional too because, in both fiction and non-fiction, the writer mixes his/her imagination with literature. As a subgenre of ethnography, feminist ethnography is a research methodology through which the ethnographers show their commitment to women and observe their plight in society over a period and discuss gender issues across society (Aune 2009, 309). From the earlier discussion, it is apparent that Dilruba Z. Ara, Tahmima Anam and Kamila Shamsie observed the lives of women of the 1971 war for a certain period and recorded their observations in their fictional narratives. Hence, it can be said that their narratives are feminist ethnographic texts. Ethnographic works by anthropologists need to be evaluated as well to maintain objectivity because, nowadays, human subject research is not free from fabrication and politics of representation. As this research aims to find women's issues connected to the 1971 war of Bangladesh in fiction and non-fiction, of Richardson's five matrixes, 'aesthetic merit' and 'impact' seem to be inappropriate here (2000). The other three matrixes have been utilised for evaluation.

Ara's novel is deeply grounded in the political context of Bangladesh in the 1960s and 1970s. She portrays the multifaceted roles of women in the nationalist politics of the 1960s and their involvement and victimisation in the 1971 war. She has acknowledged that her references to those historical events and women's untold narratives are not based on imagination but on her own experience of the war (Haque 2016). Tahmima Anam is a professional anthropologist from Harvard. Hence, her feminist intervention in the narratives of women has an anthropological connection. Though Anam does not have any physical connection to the historical struggle for Bangladesh's independence (she was born in 1975), she was brought up in an ambience rich with the memory and ideology of the Liberation War in her family. In the acknowledgements at the end of the novel, she names many of her freedom fighter friends such as Habibul Alam, Shahidullah Khan, Naila Zaman, Shireen Huq, Akhtar Ahmed, Shireen Banu, Mofidul Huq, Sultana Zaman, Colonel Nuruzzaman, Aly Zaker and Shahadat Chowdhury, along with her father and mother, who inspired her so much with their stirring tales of the 1971 war of Bangladesh that she could not help but become a writer (Anam 2007, 276). Anam's account of the female protagonist is not merely a fictional representation of war heroines in Bangladesh. Her own experience with the war narratives in her family helped her a lot to construct the framework. Anam was brought up amidst the narratives of her parents' involvement in the campaigning of the war and her grandmother's tales of the Pakistani army raiding their house and discovering the arms buried in the ground by her guerrilla uncle. All those narratives inspired the plot of *A Golden Age* (Armitstead 2016). In the context of Bangladesh, Anam's attempt to reinvestigate women's agency in the 1971 war challenges the nationalist tendencies of glorifying only male fighters and subjugating female agency in war history. Kamila Shamsie's endeavour to portray the plight of Bengali women in the context of the same war is a result of her deep connection with the life and geography of Karachi, the city where she was born and the place that always lives in her memory. Wherever she lives, she returns to Karachi again and again to write. Her first four novels are all set mainly in Karachi (Shamsie 2010). She writes, 'But wherever I lived, Karachi was the place I knew best and the place about which I wrote. I knew its subtexts, its geography, its manifestations of snobbery and patriarchy, its passions, its seasonal fruits and their different varieties' (2010). Her deep sense of geography and patriarchy helped her to sketch the lives of the Bengali women in Karachi through a heterogeneous lens. The novelists' connection to the demography, culture, and history of their respective countries suggests the 'reflexivity' of these three texts. According to Richardson, the reflexivity of the texts refers to the ethnographers' self-interest, subjectivity, self-emotion and awareness of the social events and social lives that they are writing about (2000). From the earlier discussion, we know that Ara and Anam had self-interest and personal emotions for the 1971 war because they were brought up in families and society embedded with the narratives of the war. As a close observer of the ethnic communities and women's lives in Karachi, Shamsie also shared the same emotion for marginalised Bengali women in Karachi and connected them in the cartography of struggle.

Through 'express reality', the text's connection and closeness to the truth are evaluated, though no ethnographic work aims to settle the truth (Ricardson 2000, 254). Instead, such works aim to document multiple voices for a comparative study. With a variety of genres like poetry, diary writing, linear narratives or fiction, letters, photography and so on, the postmodern approach to ethnography promotes various types of voices in a single issue but never claims to settle the truth (Aune 2009, 313). However, the important factor is how close the work of ethnography is to the truth because an ethnographer's prime ambition is to portray the hidden realities in the lives of people. Considering the novels of Dilruba Z. Ara (2015) and Tahmima Anam (2007) as feminist ethnographic fictional texts, their closeness to the truth can be verified by their approach to a few unfocused things in history like women's agency in the war and women's association with ethnic politics. The recent media coverage (Amin et al. 2016; Huda 2018) and feminist ethnographic non-fiction in oral narratives (Saikia 2011b) show women's participation in the war actively as fighters and policy makers like the fictional characters Laila, Gita (Ara 2015) and Rehana (Anam 2007). Laila and Gita's post-war plight as victims in the war resembles the post-war condition of the Birangona who were ostracised from their society and subjected to several taboos in Bangladesh where it is a matter of shame to have rape survivors in a family (D'Costa 2011; Ibrahim 2017). Anam's representation of valiant women like Rehana and Maya and their humanitarian service for the Bengali refugees in India refers to the women in Gobra Camp in India in 1971. Gobra Camp was set up in 1971 in India where Bengali women were trained to offer medical services to the Bengali freedom fighters and humanitarian services to the refugees (Saikia 2011b, 191–202). Kamila Shamsie's portrayal of the struggle of Bengali women in Karachi in the context of the 1971 war showcases the negligible position of Bengali women in Pakistan as second-class citizens and as victims of sex trafficking as per recent media intervention (Mughal and Baloch 2017; Gazdar 2003). Shamsie's text demonstrates Pakistan's silence regarding the history of the 1971 war and the successive generation's endeavour to reroute history.

Despite indicating several gender issues in the context of the 1971 Liberation War of Bangladesh, these novels cannot be taken as the representation of absolute truth because fiction is supposed to portray things aesthetically with symbols and metaphors. During the tumultuous times of genocide and gender violence in the war, the aesthetic representation of love between Laila and Santo (Ara 2015) and Rehana and the major (Anam 2015) might not be true to reality. One major reason is the shifting perspective of diasporic consciousness in the writings of these writers. Fayeza Hasanat defines the shifting perspective of the diaspora in which 'one's perceptions—of spatial and metaphysical home, identity, religion, war or memory—are always in the flux and yet dangerously alluring' (2017, 58). During the age of transnational identity, the nation has become a place of memory, desire and nostalgia for diasporic writers, and they endeavour to reconstruct the image of a nation in their writings. The treatment of the 1971 war in the narratives of Dilruba Z. Ara, Tahmima Anam and Kamila Shamsie is referred to as 'transgenerational memory' by Chatterjee (2017, 136). The homeland thus is continually recreated among the people of the successive generation who are attached to the space (136). Though these writers have travelled to their homelands several times to record the gender issues of women of the 1971 war, these writings cannot go fully beyond the personal emotions and subjectivity of the writers. So, we can mostly see courageous but defiled women in Ara's narrative, valiant women in Anam's narrative and socially ostracised women in Shamsie's narrative without many variations in their roles. Fictional narratives have a few limitations while presenting a historical account. Rather than portraying the lives, agency and suffering of the women of the 1971 war as they are, the narratives presented here offer a study mainly through symbols and metaphors. As the narrative is very conflicting, an ethnographic study on the group of women does not end with an analysis of fiction because sometimes the credibility of fiction is challenged. Sarmila Bose suggested that fiction can never be an alternative to the facts while collecting the voices of the rape victims of the 1971 war. Alternatively, their voice can be documented by interviews taken by international scholars in a systematic and verifiable manner (Bose 2007, 3871). A reading of women's issues related to their victimisation, engagement and post-war plight in several feminist ethnographic non-fictional works of the 1971 war can provide more insights into the truth.

Notes

1 'Bir Pratik' is one of the prestigious titles conferred on the valiant freedom fighters in Bangladesh by the Government of Bangladesh.

2 *Shona* is a Bengali word that means gold and is also the name of Rehana's house in *A Golden Age* (Anam 2007).

3 Bangaliyana refers to the customs and rituals of the Bengali community.

4 Naturalism was a genre of writing based on extreme realism.

5 Rabindranath Tagore (1861–1941) was a prolific Bengali poet and a Nobel laureate.

6 Pathans refer to the second largest ethnic group of Pakistan. They originally hailed from the Punjab region of Pakistan. In Kamila Shamsie's novel, Pathans are the native ethnic group of Pakistan.

7 Muhajirs refers to the largest ethnic group of Pakistan. After the Partition of 1947, Urdu-speaking Muslim people from different regions of India migrated to Pakistan and are known as Muhajirs.

8 This is a phrase used repeatedly to determine the necessity of mapping the struggle of the Third World women in Chandra Talpade Mohanty's book (2003, 43–85).

4

Women of the 1971 War in Narrative Non-fiction

> I would love to see the day when a young man or woman of this generation will come to greet me as a brave warrior, the bearer of their national flag, and the protector of their motherland. I would love to see a smile of recognition on their faces. I know it is an impossible dream, because I know that my contribution to the war and my existence as a war heroine is hidden from their knowledge. I know for sure that history has made it impossible for them to know of my existence.
>
> —Neelima Ibrahim, 'Rina's Story' in *A War Heroine, I Speak*

Introduction

Narrative non-fiction emerged as a genre of storytelling in the fields of crime investigation, medicine, science and technology in the 1990s, and it mushroomed with the advent of the 21st century due to the Internet and social media. Literature and history also took a turn during this time to shift their focus to narrative non-fiction from the traditional fictionalised narratives of war and victimisation to reveal the truth. Generally, narrative non-fiction endeavours to bring to light the true stories of the victims, but the chances of fabrication under the supervision of the editors cannot be denied. Fabrication has become a serious concern in human subject research nowadays, especially in the investigation of the cases of victims of genocide. The narratives from the sides of both victims and perpetrators are affected by fabrications, the conflicting ideologies being proof of it. The role of traditional historical narratives has always been questioned in the formation of truth because it is believed that history is always written from the perspective of rulers. The journey of narrative non-fiction started as a remedy to the shortcoming of the historical narratives. It aimed to find the truth through the representations of any true crime or horror story in newspapers and magazines. Those accounts by the victims replaced newspaper reports, catching the attention of Americans in the 1990s. With the advent of the 20th century, the emergence of journalism to report public affairs also blurred the demarcation between social science research and literary narratives, between 'true' and 'imagined' and between 'fact' and 'fiction' (Richardson and Pierre 2018, 1412). Though both fictional narratives and narrative non-fiction use the method of storytelling, they are much the same in structure and content. Fiction depends on imagination to create plots and characters. Sometimes true incidents or historical facts are taken as a source, but fiction is never liable for finding the truth. On the other hand, narrative non-fiction is dedicated to exploring the truth because the stories are supposed to be drawn from real incidents. Sometimes, rape victims in narrative non-fiction are represented anonymously or with a false identity to prevent social stigmatisation because Third World society can hardly accommodate their narratives. Jack Hart describes the structure and content of narrative non-fiction: 'Instead of sources, it would have characters. Instead of topics, it would have scenes. It would be scrupulously accurate, but it would reveal truths beyond the reach of any ordinary news report' (2011, 1).

When narrative non-fiction deals with war narratives, especially feminist narratives, oral history plays a vital role. In the sociopolitical context of our times, 'Human Rights campaigns also require that stories—especially of Rights being denied—be told' (Nayar 2016, xi). Writing life histories through the recording of interviews (with appropriate interventions of criticism and theory) has emerged as a crucial form of human rights storytelling (Smith 2011, 10). Our lives, education, upbringing and idealism are all contingent upon the narratives around us for '[w]e are born into webs of narrative:

micronarratives of familial life and macro narratives of collective identity, codes of established narratives that define our capacities to weave individual life stories' (Whitlock 2007, 11). These narratives are inseparable from history as the former owes its roots to the latter (Brüggemeier 1986, 5). Jean-Marie Schaeffer defines the tradition of oral history as '[w]ho says what in which channel to whom with what effect?' (quoted in Portelli 1998, 25). Oral history, in the form of an interview, can build vital narrative empathy because it permits the democratisation of literature. It helps to develop a discourse of human rights for a nation because 'the individual's memories in human rights texts become a subset of the national narrative with its sub-narratives of atonement, forgiveness, justice, truth, and reconciliation' (Nayar 2016, 128). Moreover, war narratives by civilians are popular forms of oral narratives. 'Since the era of air-raids, civilians have their war tales' (Portelli 1998, 27). However, the narratives of war by men and women are different in their content and approach. Men's stories are preoccupied with the heroism of the battlefield and diplomatic missions, whereas women's narratives are marked by issues related to 'health and hospital' (27). One of the reasons for such a difference is the compartmentalised lifestyles of women during wartime. Recent narratives unearth that women have participated as active fighters in many wars throughout history. Though history has typically bypassed the contributions of women, they have emerged as active soldiers in significant armed conflicts—including the Second World War, in which Soviet women participated on a large scale (Cook 2006, 543).

Feminist ethnographers depend on the oral narratives of people rather than traditional historiography to come closer to the truth or to explore those facts suppressed by history. Literary narratives throughout the world are replete with instances wherein poets and novelists have taken their resources from oral narratives in the forms of love songs, lore and memory to compose literary texts (Chamberlain and Thompson 1998, xiv). In the war-afflicted world of the 20th and 21st centuries, oral narratives narrate the untold stories of the victims of wars, often challenging the otherwise biased historical narratives of a State. Historical narratives, therefore, become an important site of gendered representation, and history as a discipline has thoroughly remained a male domain (Woolf [1929] 1977, 37–38). It has conveniently overlooked women's participation and their victimisation in wars (Cook 2006, xxvii). From this perspective, the Liberation War of Bangladesh of 1971 is one of the cruellest wars in world history. The history of the Liberation War is preoccupied with the heroism of the Muktibahini, but the narratives of raped women and women fighters have been largely ignored in the State-sponsored historiographies of Bangladesh (Hossain 2012). Even the records of the International Crimes Tribunal, which was established in 1993 to seek international justice for the victims, are often mute about these women victims (Linton 2010a, 187). In the post-war period, Sheikh Mujibur Rahman, the then prime minister of Bangladesh, honoured the women who survived sexual violence with the title 'Birangona' to acknowledge their contribution to the freedom struggle (Murshed 1997, 120). However, this recognition did not help them as they still faced social prejudices, hatred and ignorance from their fellow citizens (Mamoon 2017, 15). As an initiative by Sheikh Mujibur Rahman, Birangona were trained and made fit for jobs depending on their aptitude and qualification by the Bangladesh Women's Rehabilitation Board. Bangladesh went through political turmoil even after the war ended, and it reached its worst point in 1975 when Sheikh Mujibur Rahman and his family were assassinated.

Narrative non-fiction has become a weapon for feminist ethnographers who have endeavoured to deconstruct the gendered nature of war history through women's oral narratives to reinvestigate the truth behind war crimes, genocide and gendered violence. The Bangladesh Liberation War of 1971 is a confusing chapter of world history due to the conflicting narratives of war crimes and victimisation. The fifteen-volume manuscript of the Liberation War (titled in Bengali as *Bangladesher Shadhinota Juddha: Dolilpotro*)

([1982] 2009) only concentrates on the genocide and mass rape during the nine months of the freedom struggle. Even though the eighth volume of this book accommodates the narratives of sweepers, lower-ranked policemen and morgue workers, it could only accommodate the narratives of five rape survivors (Mookherjee 2015b, 180). The national narratives of Bangladesh as well as several historical sources say that over 3,000,000 people were brutally killed and 200,000 to 400,000 women were raped by the allied force of the Pakistani army and pro-Pakistani Razakars (Linton 2010b, 194). When the International Crimes Tribunal was set up in 1993 to seek international justice for genocidal violence and rape, it could produce no record of the gendered violence that happened in Bangladesh (Linton 2010a, 187). So it has always remained a very tough task to figure out the facts regarding the gendered violence that happened in Bangladesh in 1971. The fictional narratives and popular media on the Liberation War of Bangladesh are preoccupied with the tales of heroism, sacrifice, bloodshed, death and survival of the Muktibahini. At the same time, the post-war narratives avoid the tales of rape, sexual harassment and subjugation of women in Bangladesh during the war even though many academics attested that rape was an important weapon in the genocide (Hossain 2012). The conflict of narratives, especially victims' narratives, has raised the question of their authenticity many times. Even the debate was on both the claim of authenticity and the scope of fabrication. Though the ethnic conflict between Pakistan and Bangladesh is discussed with much importance in history, the domestic struggle of the women in the country has been completely neglected (Saikia 2004, 275). The politics of patriarchal representation suppresses their voice in mainstream historiography. Stuart J. Hall suggests that meaning is always produced through representation; the intentional and constructionist approaches create a discursive image of something (1997). Postcolonial historiography also suffers from such politics of representation through which women's voices, their roles and their agency are silenced or produced with a discursive image. The main reason behind this is the lack of women's voices. If women have their voice, bypassing the politics of representation, they can speak for themselves (Spivak 1988, 25). Feminist ethnographers of the postcolonial age have endeavoured to bring out the women's voices in their narrative non-fiction so that women can bypass the politics of patriarchal representation in history.

The oral narratives of the Birangona are manyfold in different feminist ethnographic non-fiction works. However, the sustained and relentless efforts of Neelima Ibrahim, a literary scholar, professor of the University of Dhaka and social worker, to give these women a voice have resulted in recording the narratives of rape survivors whom she visited during their rehabilitation process in 1972. When she met the rape survivors and reached out to support and empower them, they shared their tales of suffering and experiences of prejudice with her. Ibrahim recorded the accounts of approximately thirty to forty women, and from those, she selected seven to compile her book *Aami Birangona Balchi* (first published in Bengali in 1994). The year 2011 was important for Bangladesh because the country completed forty years of independence. In the same year, a few feminist ethnographers and historians of South Asia and its diaspora published their ethnographic non-fiction that changed the scenario of academic research on the *Muktijoddha* (the Liberation War of Bangladesh). In 2011, Yasmin Saikia, Bina D'Costa and Sarmila Bose presented oral narratives directly from the Bengali and non-Bengali victims of the 1971 war and rediscovered the gender issues related to the war. Nayanika Mookherjee also published her book in 2015, following the same feminist track of bringing the oral history of victims into ethnographic literature. Recent studies have shown plenty of instances of gender crime based on the ethnic politics between Bengali-speaking and Urdu-speaking people (Saikia 2011b; Bose 2011a; Ranjan 2016). The most notable is the rape of thousands of Bihari women by Bengali nationalists after the end of the 1971 war.

Building its framework upon human subject research and contemporary human rights discourse, this chapter attempts to reconstruct the traditional historiography of the 1971 war from a feminist point of view, using illustrations from feminist ethnographic non-fiction by Ibrahim (2017), Mookherjee (2015b), Bose (2011a) and Saikia (2011b). Based on the theoretical framework of feminist ethnographers such as Sanjukta Ghosh (2016), Kristin Aune (2009) and Kamala Visweswaran (1994), this chapter also points out the necessity of feminist ethnography for a culturally relative and contextual study of the lives of women who were involved in the war. Utilising the concept of noted postcolonial feminist Gayatri Chakraborty Spivak that the subaltern can speak if they can bypass the politics of representation (1988, 25), this chapter elaborates the endeavours of a few feminist ethnographers to make the subaltern voice public, opposing the patriarchal representation of women in the history of the 1971 war. The Birangona and their role in making Bangladesh are elaborated with references from the feminist ethnographic literature of Neelima Ibrahim's *A War Heroine, I Speak* (2017, translated from the 1994 Bengali text *Aami Birangona Balchi*) and Nayanika Mookherjee's *The Spectral Wound: Sexual Violence, Public Memories and the Bangladesh war of 1971* (2015b). The following section covers the victimisation of non-Bengali people, particularly non-Bengali women, by Bengali nationalists after the 1971 war, drawing illustrations from the narratives of Sarmila Bose's *Dead Reckoning: Memories of the 1971 Bangladesh War* (2011a) and Yasmin Saikia's *Women, War, and the Making of Bangladesh: Remembering 1971* (2011b). This chapter also evaluates women's location in the unknown register of the archive of the 1971 war through the references in Saikia's book, which contains the narratives of the real survivors of the wars: the women who tell their stories as 'agents of change, as social workers, caregivers, and wartime fighters' (Saikia 2011b, Synopsis). This chapter ends by validating the claims made by the authors with sources like interviews, newspaper articles and counter-narratives. It also evaluates these four texts as feminist ethnographic texts followed by the evaluation of ethnography through Richardson's model (2000).

The Birangona and Bangladesh

The Birangona emerged as courageous women in the popular culture of Bangladesh after the war ended, but their title did not bring them the honour they deserve. They sacrificed as much as their male counterparts, but unlike the men, their voices are silenced and they are marginalised. The post-independent public memory of the representation of the Birangona has hardly been complemented by their real suffering until 1990 when the oral history of these women started to be documented (Mookherjee 2015b, 14). After the war, many Birangona fled with their Pakistani abusers to escape the shame of being unwanted in the country in which they dreamed of living (Ibrahim 2017, 38). Even when the brutality of war ceased in the country, brutality towards the Birangona continued. Many families in Bangladesh killed their abducted daughters to rid themselves of the shame, and few of them excommunicated the rape survivors (D'Costa 2011, 195). The exact number of Birangona, their role in the historical war and their plight in postcolonial Bangladesh have remained controversial issues of discussion for almost half a century. It took more than two decades to come up with the oral narratives of real Birangona because the sociopolitical conditions in Bangladesh were not favourable enough to accommodate their heroic deeds. Neelima Ibrahim's *Aami Birangona Balchi* (A War Heroine, I Speak) was the beginning of a genre that revolutionised not only the genre of storytelling but also the feminist way of revisiting history (2017). After Ibrahim's book was published, a few other South Asian authors and scholars have also worked on the narratives of the Birangona, with an estimated 200 to 300 narratives already recorded (Mamoon 2017, 15).

However, these narratives have faced their share of criticism. Their authenticity was challenged, and critics questioned the role of the academics, historians, interviewers and editors in the documentation of these narratives. Rigoberta Menchú, Binjamin Wilkomirski and, recently, Sarmila Bose have been accused on more than one occasion of fabricating victims' narratives. Rigoberta Menchú, a memoirist who recorded the killing of her family members along with other Mayan Indians by the Guatemalan army, was charged with fabricating her narratives. Her claim of being an eyewitness to the event was vehemently challenged by establishing that she lived far away in a Mexican school at the time of the genocide (Peskin 2000, 39). Similarly, the documentation of gendered violence in the Liberation War of Bangladesh by Sarmila Bose is allegedly inauthentic and unreliable (2011a). Bose's claims were dismissed by most academicians. Nayanika Mookherjee wrote, 'To take Bose's word for it would be an unfortunate misreading' (2011). Neelima Ibrahim's account of the Birangona remains one of the most cited works among the works of successive writers dealing with the gendered violence of the 1971 war (2017). Noted academic works by Mookherjee, Saikia and Bose on the rape victims of the war cite Ibrahim's book on many occasions.

A War Heroine, I Speak recounts the struggle and survival of seven rape victims of the 1971 war in Bangladesh (Ibrahim 2017). Ibrahim's narratives resurrect the significant role of women in the otherwise suppressed tales of the Liberation War. She was successful to a certain extent in showcasing women's equal participation and questioning the unequal treatment women received during and after the war. While men were honoured for their heroism, women were nothing more than objects of pity. Commenting on their state, Ibrahim says that the citizens would have preferred to find the violated women dead rather than living and breathing (2017, 57). However, being a social worker and humanitarian, she believed that the Birangona have the right to live with dignity in their free country. She strived for the empowerment of the raped women because '[w]omen form an essential half of any society, even in conflict' (Karam 2000, 2). The narratives in *A War Heroine, I Speak* deal 'not merely with the wrongs done to the women in 1971 but the way they try to rebuild the lives afterwards, sometimes abetted by a few humane people they come across, but sometimes slighted and insulted by some unfeeling ones' (Ibrahim 2017, ix). Fayeza Hasanat of the University of Central Florida, Orlando, translated the book into English and published it in 2017 so that it could attain global exposure. The translated version contains major structural changes. The translator has subdivided the chapters and titled them, unlike the spontaneous narratives of the Bengali version. The narratives, which are derived from several interviews, use fictional names because going public with the names of the rape survivors may negatively affect the social life of the Birangona.

The first chapter of the book introduces Tara Nielsen, a Birangona who migrated to Holland after being displaced from her own country, independent Bangladesh. Neelima Ibrahim met her at a dinner party in Copenhagen where she had gone to attend the annual board meeting of the International Alliance of Women (Ibrahim 2017, 3). Within a few minutes of conversing with her, Ibrahim recognised that she was Tara Banerjee, a Hindu girl from Bangladesh. She had met her in the operation theatre at the rehabilitation centre. Tara was kidnapped and raped by her fellow countrymen and then handed over to the Pakistani military for prolonged torture. The brutality towards Tara continued in the military camp till 16 December, the day of Bangladesh's victory over Pakistan. During the war, Bangladeshi women were not only victimised by the Pakistani military but also kidnapped and raped by pro-Pakistani Bengalis and Bengali nationalists (Saikia 2004, 279–281). In the words of Tara:

> The first man to brutalize me physically in that hospital was a Bengali. I was too weak to fight back and too shocked to absorb the truth that

> a Bengali man had violated my honor instead of trying to save me. My head was not strong yet, and my body lay powerless, as I was being dishonored by a bestial Bengali man. (Ibrahim 2017, 11)

After her abduction, Tara escaped from her nation and migrated to Holland. There she became a nurse and married a doctor to live a dignified life.

The sixth narrative, 'Fatema's Story', talks of Chapa, another Hindu girl who met the same fate, but she was not fortunate enough to escape from the country. Her father was a rebel in the Language Movement of 1952 in East Pakistan, and her elder brother also joined the freedom struggle. After losing her family in the war, she was raped by hundreds of Pakistani soldiers. Her suffering continued even after independence in 1971 when neither her family's sacrifice nor her suffering was recognised by the nation. Her only identity was that she was a Hindu girl raped by Muslims, and hence, she was ostracised in society (Ibrahim 2017, 121). The portrayal of victims' plights in literature by Neelima Ibrahim, Nayanika Mookherjee, Yasmin Saikia, Tahmima Anam and others indicates that nine months of physical abuse and psychological torture in the lives of the raped women were followed by their struggle for identity in a free state. Hence, they were left with the option of either migration or suicide. This helplessness and pain of the Birangona in the present time has started to appear in contemporary scholarship on migration and communal relations in Bangladesh. Mookherjee states that in various texts, particularly, the hair photograph (see Chapter 1), and all forms of public narrativisation, 'the figure of the birangona lingers for its contemporary audiences so as to repeat their presence and refuse to let this violent encounter be the past' (2015a, 388).

Migration for the sake of gaining an identity, a vital postcolonial stance, is apparent in Ibrahim's narratives. If the Birangona migrated during the war for the sake of their lives and chastity, then, after the war, they migrated to Pakistan, India and other countries to reclaim their identity from the position of defiled women. In her narrative, Ibrahim recounts the experience of thirty rape survivors who moved to Pakistan with their abusers instead of staying in the country because '[a] home was not a place for a woman whose body was used by hundreds of men' (Ibrahim 2017, 41). The second chapter of *A War Heroine, I Speak*, titled 'Meher Jan Speaks', narrates the heart-wrenching story of a fourteen-year-old girl who was raped for nine months in a military camp. Following her victimisation, she migrated to Pakistan with one of her rapists only to restore a dignified identity. When Neelima Ibrahim approached her and asked her to stay in Bangladesh, she was mature enough to foresee her plight and suffering in her own country. Hence, she decided to migrate to Pakistan after marrying her sixty-year-old rapist to avoid being pushed into a corner. Meher told Neelima:

> I was young in age, but my experience had already told me that there would be no peace or happiness for me in the new country; no one would stand by me. No one came to save me the day these brutes abducted me from my own house; in fact, people from my village helped these animals to collect us as one of their sex toys. (37)

After the war ended and during the resolution process, women continued to be treated as sex objects because men do not easily let go of the brutal behaviour learnt in wartime. Women who had been very courageous fighters and peacemakers during the war in different areas of Africa and Asia were victimised in a war-torn society by their men (Meintjes 2011, 4–5). Ibrahim's narratives refer to Bengali women who were physically and psychologically tortured after they returned from their war imprisonment. In the seventh narrative of Ibrahim's *A War Heroine, I Speak*, Mina, a Birangona, was blamed and driven out of her home by her husband who accused her of being violated by the Pakistanis (2017, Chapter 7). Women became soft and vulnerable targets in every conflict in Bangladesh, be it sociopolitical, gendered or ethnic.

A huge number of Biharis migrated to East Pakistan after the Partition of 1947, and they supported the Pakistani perpetrators of the 1971 genocide due to religious and ethnic connections (Saikia 2004, 275). The sixth narrative in Ibrahim's book highlights the survival strategy of Fatema, a victim of the ethnic conflict between the Bengali and the Bihari community during the 1971 war. Fatema was a free-spirited girl in Khulna and was raised by a radical religious group primarily led by Biharis living in East Pakistan. The intensity of violence imposed upon her by the allied groups of pro-Pakistani Bengalis, Biharis and the Pakistani military is narrated in the following lines:

> Nasir Ali snatched my little brother from me and thrashed him on the street. I heard Pona crying for help, and then I saw his skull break into pieces. My brother's brain jumped out of his tiny head and fell like a lump of blood on the pavement. Nasir and his team dragged me towards their housing estate … Nasir Ali and his father took turns in raping me and then handed me over to other men of their community. (Ibrahim 2017, 117)

Such references to ethnic conflicts between Urdu-speaking Biharis and Bengali-speaking Bangladeshis became a controversial issue in the successive narratives by academicians such as Yasmin Saikia and Sarmila Bose. Saikia and Bose documented a kind of counter-narrative of Bihari women in their respective books *Women, War and the Making of Bangladesh: Remembering 1971* (2011b) and *Dead Reckoning: Memories of the 1971 Bangladesh War* (2011a) to show that Bihari women were also victimised by Bengali nationalists in Bangladesh after the end of the 1971 war.

After the war, the abducted women in Pakistani military camps were rescued by the joint force of the Indian Army and Bengali nationalists. The victory slogan 'Joy Bangla'[1] could not provide any solace to the women who endured savage torture for nine months in those camps. Their compatriots were not proud of their courage. On the contrary, they were ashamed of their being alive. Ibrahim's narratives detail the concerns of the citizens in a free nation regarding their war heroines. On the day of the victory, the nation glorified the deeds of the male freedom fighters, but it conveniently denied the contribution of the war heroines as co-warriors (Ibrahim 2017, 57). Neelima Ibrahim, in the third narrative of *A War Heroine, I Speak*, discusses the crisis of identity of a Birangona named Rina in postcolonial Bangladesh (2017, 56–75). During wartime, a Bengali woman was thought to be dignified if she was a personal attendant to an army officer. Rina, being an educated, pretty and smart girl, became the personal sex slave of an officer and submitted to his greed because she felt that it was better to endure one man's lust than to be abducted by a group of hungry beasts. Rina was attacked publicly by Bengali people, even by a group of little Bengali boys once, with her new identity being a 'Bengali whore'. She then knew that her fate was that of Lady Macbeth's. She laments, 'All the perfumes of Arabia were not enough to cover my crime' (60–61). Rina, like Meher Jan, decided to escape to Pakistan to get rid of this shame. When Ibrahim tried to persuade her to stay, she declared: 'I would rather go to Pakistan and spend the rest of my shame-filled life with these monsters. Handling these animals would be easier than confronting my loved ones' (64). In the fourth narrative, titled 'Shefali's Story', the Birangona appears to be excommunicated, mute, silent and marginalised. According to the narrative, their presence in a marriage ceremony was considered inauspicious (86). Such a representation of the valiant women of the 1971 war shows that the nation's independence brought honour and dignity to the male freedom fighters and also allowed the people who fled like cowards to save themselves. At the same time, it bore no fruit for the Birangona, who sacrificed the most (69).

The narratives of the rape survivors documented by Neelima Ibrahim not only represent the stories of the struggle of the Birangona but also talk about contemporary social and political movements in Bangladesh. The genocide in Dhaka that took place on 25 March 1971 and the imprisonment of thousands of intellectuals and women are topics discussed in this book. Most of the rape victims were kidnapped by the Pakistani military (associated with the pro-Pakistanis) in the darkness of the night (Ibrahim 2017, 78). The general elections of 1970, Mujib's victory, the Agartala Conspiracy Case, Mujib's imprisonment, the freedom struggle, independence and Mujib's assassination in 1975—all are discussed in fragmented narratives. In post-war Bangladesh, the Birangona observed that the local perpetrators escaped punishment and claimed that they were the saviours of the nation by joining local politics (84). In the fifth chapter, 'Mayna's Tale', the narrator shamefully observes how the treacherous Bengali people or Razakars hid behind the mask of patriotism and shouted the slogan 'Joy Bangla' (101).

Ibrahim's narratives also focus on the transformation of the rape survivors into courageous ladies, social workers and unacknowledged heroes of the nation. Despite being raped, victimised, discriminated against, displaced and threatened, these women dared to bring about a change in society. Unlike the usual war narratives, Ibrahim's narratives are not always gloomy. Instead, these narratives occasionally represent the glorious sides of humanity during and after the war. The Partition of 1947, which divided India and Pakistan, took place on account of the religious identity of the majority of the people in either country. However, Bangladesh defied the notion of religion being the only identity and proved that culture and ethnicity could also be major identity markers. When the post-Partition society of South Asia was preoccupied with hate politics, the bonding between the Hindus and the Muslims in Ibrahim's narratives is extreme. One such instance is of a Hindu rape victim Shefa who named her son Jogi to remember the generosity of the Indian soldier Joginder who called her mother after rescuing her from the den of the Pakistani military (Ibrahim 2017, 82). War brought Fatema and Chapa together as caring sisters in a relationship beyond their religious beliefs, and to Fatema's mother, Chapa became another daughter and the replacement for Fatema's dead brother (122). The narratives of the women who experienced sexual violence, such as those of Tara, Mayna and Fatema, mention a few kind-hearted Bengali men who strongly supported them, married them and helped them to build their identities. Neelima Ibrahim herself, Moshfeka Mahmud (the director of the rehabilitation centre), the attending doctors, the nurses and many other social workers came together to rehabilitate the rape survivors through treatment, abortion, adoption of the war babies, education, empowerment and employment. Bangabandhu Sheikh Mujibur Rahman, the founder-father of the nation, was dedicated to the concerns of the Birangona and called them 'brave mothers' (18).

Nayanika Mookherjee's *The Spectral Wound: Sexual Violence, Public Memories, and the Bangladesh War of 1971* is another important and scholarly book dealing with the lives of the Birangona (2015b). After the end of the Liberation War of Bangladesh, many scholars endeavoured to interview the Birangona in post-conflict Bangladesh. Over 300 to 400 victims' narratives could be recorded up to 2017 (Mamoon 2017, 15). Mookherjee's narratives are set apart from the others because these deal with the plight of the Birangona in contemporary Bangladesh with a claim that the previous narratives could hardly accommodate their real experiences (Mookherjee 2015b, 14). Mookherjee faced several questions from 'NGO activists, human rights lawyers, intellectuals, writers, journalists, academics, feminists' regarding the contemporary lives of the Birangona; most of those were about their conjugal lives, acceptance and plights (xix). However, Mookherjee affirmed to them that the Birangona continued to be married to their husbands just as they had been before. She also focuses on the limitations of a few literary and cultural representations in which these war heroines are shown to be 'abnormal' and marginalised (xix). She writes of Shiromoni, an artist in Bangladesh, who was courageous enough to share her story of rape by Pakistani officials and Bengali collaborators. According to Mookherjee, 'Shiromoni dismantled the prevalent stereotype that all birangonas are ashamed and invisible as a result of their rape' (xix).

The aesthetic representation of the Birangona and their connection to the truth in the 1971 war are frequently discussed topics in Mookherjee's book. In popular culture, like TV, films, photographs, advertisements and others, Mookherjee claims that the Birangona are represented in three ways: first, there is the corporeal Birangona, who provides an insight into her horrific life filled with the trauma of violence. Second, Mookherjee talks about the representations in performative domains such as literature and visual culture where they are presented ambiguously or made to exit from the narrative. Third, the national consciousness of Bangladesh regarding the Birangona is discussed. The nation still feels an erotic attraction to this subject (Mookherjee 2015b, 178–179). The visual representation of the Birangona constitutes a larger part of Mookherjee's narratives. Mookherjee talks about photographs by the famous photographers of South Asia, including Indian photojournalist Kishore Parekh and Bangladeshi photographer Rashid Talukder, whose images of the Birangona exhibit the emotions of raped women in the war through the 'lone tear, watery eyes, covered faces, and sideways, downward glances' (188). The most discussed image in Mookherjee's book is the famous hair photograph by well-known Bangladeshi photographer Naibuddin Ahmed. The photo shows a Birangona hiding behind her long hair in shame, unwanted and deserted (xvi–xvii). Naibuddin's photograph was published in the *Washington Post* in 1971, causing a vehement public outburst regarding the gendered crimes in the 1971 war (189–190). This horrific image reconstructed public consciousness regarding the rape survivors who started to be unwanted, despised and marginalised in free Bangladesh, the country that was born out of their chastity. Though Mookherjee acknowledges that a photograph speaks more than a painting, Naibuddin Ahmed's symbolic photograph cannot encapsulate the happenings in the lives of real Birangona (192). Mookherjee describes the lives of the Birangona just after the independence of Bangladesh under the reign of Sheikh

Mujibur Rahman, the founder-president of Bangladesh. Many steps were taken, including the rehabilitation of the women through work opportunities and education, their shelter in the rehabilitation camps and their recognition as Birangona or 'brave heroine of the war'. Newspapers published images of prosperous women in neat and clean dresses with oiled hair engaging in different activities in the rehabilitation centres. Mookherjee, however, claims that these images are non-individualised and generic and do not portray their real status (199). The images presented in a post-war advertisement of a nationalised bank and a cosmetics company in Bangladesh feature in Mookherjee's book. She asserts that these advertisements are fictional representations of the Birangona, and their bodies are aestheticised and commodified in such representations (199–201).

In Mookherjee's book, the narrative of Chaya Rani Dutta, a sex worker in a Bangladeshi red-light area, unearths many hidden truths of gendered violence in 1971 (2015b, 235–238). During the war, Chaya was only fifteen or sixteen years old, a fatherless girl accompanied by her mother. Chaya married an Indian but abandoned him before the 1971 war to come back to her mother, who died in the same year. Her house was looted, and the villagers swindled her out of her wealth. One day, she escaped to the jungle with her Hindu neighbour after hearing of the arrival of the Pakistani military in their village. Notably, being Hindu, Chaya could not be given shelter during wartime because Hindus were the soft targets of the Pakistani army (236). Chaya was caught by the Bengali collaborators popularly known as Razakars. She was raped by four to five men. 'At that point, Chaya said, she felt she was a *kolonkini* (stained person) and wondered whether she should die. However, it was not easy to die, and she reasoned that the rape was not her fault' (236). After the war, Chaya struggled to seek food and shelter as a war heroine in a war-torn country. 'People would respect and help her since she was a woman trying to earn a living on her own' (236). She took a job as a cook and later married a Muslim man but remained unacceptable to his family as she was an orphan and had worked as a hotel cook. Her husband supported her, but he was compelled to drive her away due to social and economic pressure. Finally, Chaya ended her journey in Tanbajar in 1979, accepting prostitution as a means of living. At least no one would approach her there to scrap her freedom to live in this free country. She met various types of people there, and 'this place gave her the sense of security that the polite facade of normal life cannot give a single woman' (237). She married a Hindu client of hers, but again her married life was doomed as her husband was murdered due to some business affairs. So she had to return to the brothel again to get shelter, this time as a senior guardian. Mookherjee documents the experience of a few women like Chaya whose marital and social lives were affected by the gendered violence of the 1971 war (Lambek 2016, 1002).

Citing Yasmin Saikia, Nayanika Mookherjee criticises the dehumanisation of Bihari women in Bangladeshi narratives, especially in *Bangladesher Shadhinota Juddha: Dolilpotro* (a set of historical deeds preserved by the Government of Bangladesh) ([1982] 2009), where Bihari women are not shown as beautiful or intelligent (2015b, 180). One thing that needs to be mentioned is Mookherjee's non-engagement in portraying the plights of Bihari women who were also been victimised after the end of the 1971 war. The Bihari community mostly appears in Mookherjee's book as the collaborators of the Pakistani army in crime, and they are jointly referred to with the Bengali collaborators as Razakars (8, 190). Mookherjee shows that during wartime, Bengali women were not only violated by the Pakistani military but also subjugated by their Bengali co-workers, Pakistani officers and Bihari employees (229). She acknowledges that the narratives of the victimisation of Bihari women have gone unaccounted for decades and were recently addressed by feminist writers and activists beyond Bangladesh such as Yasmin Saikia (23, 36, 133).

Nayanika Mookherjee takes a postcolonial feminist ethnographic approach to interpret the lives of the rape victims of the 1971 war. The role of a feminist ethnographer is to go for a heterogenised and context-specific study of the lives of women (Visweswaran 1994, 20). Unlike

Western feminists and many South Asian feminists, Mookherjee shows that the experience of all the victims is not the same; they can neither be simply tagged as marginalised for being raped nor they can be shown as glorified war heroines. The narrative of Kajoli shows the subjugation of women in a patriarchal society where women are thought to be unable to tell even their own stories of victimisation (Mookherjee 2015b, 78–79). At the same time, Mookherjee showcases the narratives of Birangona such as Shiromoni to show that not all rape victims are afraid of public exposure (xix, 214). Unlike traditional Bengali narratives, Mookherjee's account is multidimensional because Pakistani officers are not always rapists here. Sometimes, they appear as the saviours of a Bengali girl who was continuously victimised in her own country by her employer (229). While the raped women of the 1971 war are generally represented as ostracised from their families, Mookherjee mentions the instances in which many raped women have continued to be married after the war, and their husbands support them despite knowing of their victimisation (xx). The story of Chaya Rani Dutta shows the struggle of a rape victim in independent Bangladesh where she had to negotiate her life, livelihood, survival and death.

Nayanika Mookherjee has done a praiseworthy job in collecting the stories of real Birangona, not an easy task in the 1990s when communal tension was surging throughout Bangladesh as a consequence of the Babri Mosque demolition incident in India. Mookherjee's book has created a strong impact on the public consciousness and popular culture of Bangladesh and beyond regarding the truth of genocide and rape in the 1971 war. In the 'Postscript' section, Mookherjee shows how the lives of the Birangona are not always as gloomy as presented by most writers and historians. She shows that the new Bangladesh has started to acknowledge the women's agency in the 1971 war. In 2007, eight Birangona were invited to inaugurate the Victory Day programme in Dhaka, the first time when the nation thought of them not merely as Birangona but as *Muktijoddha* (Mookherjee 2015b, 268).

Recent Bangladeshi documentaries, films and television serials have started to depict the characters of Birangona not as shameful beings but as active agents behind the birth of Bangladesh (268). The testimonies of three Birangona from Enayetpur, an eastern village of Bangladesh, strengthened the process of trial and punishment of Ghulam Azam, who was accused of being engaged in the mass rape and genocide in the 1971 war (Mookherjee 2015b, 39).

Neelima Ibrahim's and Nayanika Mookherjee's works on the lives of the Birangona are significant not only in their contexts but also for further academic research on the 1971 war in Bangladesh. Their method of collecting the oral history of rape victims can be sorted as feminist ethnography based on the elaboration of the methods of noted contemporary feminist ethnographers. Feminist ethnography is a method of studying women's lived experiences over time from the commitment to those women. It also elaborates on the power structure among women of different ethnic groups in society (Aune 2009; Ghosh 2016; Visweswaran 1994). Oral narratives in Neelima Ibrahim's *A War Heroine, I Speak* unearth the untold stories of marginalised women of the 1971 war. With opportunities to voice their suffering, they have restructured the course of traditional historiography where women have had little representation. According to Spivak, if the problem of representation can be sidelined through support and opportunity, the marginalised and the oppressed can speak for themselves (1988, 25). Ibrahim's portrayal of the suffering of humanity proves that 'any life story, whether a written autobiography or an oral testimony, is shaped not only by the reworkings of experience through memory and re-evaluation but also always at least to some extent by art' (Chamberlain and Thompson 1998, 1). The dignified voice of Rina, a Birangona, shows the courage and spirit the women still have after enduring a series of physical and mental torments: 'I am a woman warrior, and no coward can have me!' (Ibrahim 2017, 71). Along with the stories of suffering, prejudices and pervasive silence, other vital points of Ibrahim's narratives are the showcasing of women empowerment and

Hindu–Muslim unity in a war-torn country. The narratives speak of the dreams of acceptance in the country for which the victims sacrificed their youth, chastity, family and belongings. Despite the hurdles they continuously face and the silence brooding over their life, a war heroine still dares to say: 'I will still keep dreaming that, one day, they will recognize me, not as a victim of the war, but as a brave hero' (75).

Neelima Ibrahim's feminist ethnographic literature meets many of the criteria defined by Richardson (2000). As a piece of ethnographic work, Ibrahim's contribution is 'substantive' because it is completely grounded in the context of the 1971 war and its aftermath. She was a social worker during and after the 1971 war and contributed a lot to the rehabilitation of the rape survivors of the war. She interviewed the rape victims whom she came in contact with during her social work. Mookherjee's work is also grounded within the context of 1990s Bangladesh when the country went through extreme political turmoil and sectarian violence. Her work is substantive because she grounded the lives of the Birangona within the context when Bangladesh was at a crucial juncture of rising religious fundamentalism. Both Ibrahim's and Mookherjee's works are 'reflexive', another matrix of Richardson (2000), because they were aware of the happenings of the war and undertook the projects of documenting the lives of the Birangona. Muecke discusses the role of language behind the credibility of ethnographic work (1994). An ethnographer's credibility depends on the access to the language used by the informants, and if the language is different, an interpreter can help (Muecke 1994, 192). Language and ethnicity were advantageous for Ibrahim and Mookherjee, both hailing from Bengali families, to study the women they were covering. Ibrahim was an activist in the rehabilitation process. The connection of Ibrahim's and Mookherjee's works to reality, termed by Richardson (2000) as 'express reality', is apparent because other feminist ethnographic non-fiction works like those by Bina D'Costa (2011) and Yasmin Saikia (2011b) also portray such dehumanisation of the

Birangona in Bangladesh and their status as defiled and unwanted women there. Despite being the first authenticated version of the narratives of the victims of the 1971 war, Ibrahim's narratives have a few shortcomings. The issues uncovered in Ibrahim's narratives are violence against women during the peace process, women's agency in post-war conflicts, victimisation of non-Bengali Bihari women in Bangladesh and women's active participation in the armed conflict. In the contemporary global context, women contribute to war and play significant roles in the peace process in the aftermath of the war. The United Nations recognised the presence of such women in peacemaking, and the United Nations Security Council Resolution 1325 on 'Women, Peace and Security' was passed in 2000 (Nanda 2018, 21). Ibrahim's narratives ignore certain positive sides of women's agency in the war and have hardly any instances of women bearing weapons and being directly involved in the freedom struggle. The year 1971 was remarkable in the history of South Asia due to women's agency in two major conflicts: the Naxalbari conflict in India and the Liberation War in Bangladesh (Roy 2019). Recent fictional narratives such as Tahmima Anam's novel *A Golden Age* (2007) and Dilruba Z. Ara's *Blame* (2015) show women as active participants in the armed conflict and not merely as victims. Tareq Masud's documentary *Muktir Katha* is a tale of the heroism of women freedom fighters in the 1971 war in a remote village in Faridpur District of Bangladesh (Masud and Masud 1999). These films and novels are based on the real-life narratives of women who were directly associated with the 1971 war but were swept under the rug of mainstream historiography. Another gap in Ibrahim's and Mookherjee's narratives is that they document the struggle of Bengali women in the 1971 war in particular and not the struggle of women in general. When recent studies by Bangladeshi as well as international academicians such as Dilruba Z. Ara (2015), Yasmin Saikia (2011b) and Sarmila Bose (2011a) clearly state that Bihari women were also victimised by Bengali nationalists for vengeance after the end of the war in Bangladesh, one wonders why

Ibrahim's narratives remain silent about this. Though Mookherjee's narratives do not engage with the Bihari women and their stateless dehumanised condition in Bangladesh, she acknowledges that these are serious issues that need to be covered.

Non-Bengali Rape Victims of the 1971 War

Several post-2000 narrative non-fictional works by South Asian authors claim that the traditional historiography related to the 1971 war is one-sided and biased (Bose 2011a; Saikia 2011b). The narratives of Ibrahim and Mookherjee are broadly based on the survival strategies of the Birangona in/after the 1971 war, but Saikia and Bose focus on a completely different side. They claim that Bengali nationalists were also perpetrators of violence when the 1971 war is seen through the lens of gendered violence rather than ethnic clash. Crimes against humanity were committed by both sides in that gendered violence: the Pakistani military raped and tortured Bengali women during the war, and Bengali nationalists raped non-Bengali Bihari women after the war as revenge (Saikia 2004, 275). Sarmila Bose's *Dead Reckoning: Memory of the 1971 Bangladesh War* presents a conflicting version of the truth about the genocidal violence and rape in the 1971 war (2011a). Bose, an American journalist of Indian origin and the grandniece of Netaji Subhas Chandra Bose, asserts that the claims of Bengalis about the number of casualties and rapes are purely exaggerated, 'distorted versions of actual events' and 'pure fabrication' (2011a, 164). Bose interviewed not only the victims but also the Pakistani army personnel who were in Bangladesh during the Liberation War. She claims that the accounts of violence and rape in the 1971 war by several witnesses including the memoirists Jahanara Alam, Nurul Ula, Kaliranjan Shil, Imamuz Zaman, Neelima Ibrahim and others lack 'adequate authentication or verification process to filter claims made by contributors; as a result, there is significant variation in the quality and reliability of contributions'

(197). Bose's narratives dismiss a few claims made by historians and writers of the 1971 war. One of them is the sectarian violence against the Hindus who were supposed to be special targets in the genocide. The narrative of a Hindu survivor Nitai Gayan has been put in words in Bose's book: 'They did not shoot us because we were Hindu, but because we were their enemy; we were going to return, and we were not going to return empty-handed' (123–124). Based on her interview with retired Pakistani officers who were in East Pakistan in 1971, Bose claims that Pakistani officers and their families also faced brutalities at the hands of Bengalis during the war but such incidents are denied in Bangladesh's account of the Liberation War. She refers to Mymensingh, a city in Bangladesh where many Pakistani officers and their families were brutally murdered in the army cantonment. Based on the eyewitness accounts of two locals named Mohammad Abdul Haque and Sheikh Sultan Ahmed, Bose writes, '100 Pakistani officers were killed ... women and children were killed by the Bengalis, and some women were raped and killed or abducted' (84). The victimisation of the Bihari community by Bengali nationalists has also received special priority in Bose's writing. The narratives of Bihari victims claim that over 3,000 or 4,000 Bihari families became fatherless and shelterless during the war resolution process in the ethnic cleansing performed by Bengali nationalists (143).

Bihari people's victimisation in independent Bangladesh is a matter of discussion in recent academia. A large number of Bihari people migrated from the Indian state of Bihar to Bangladesh after the 1947 Partition because it was easier for them to move to East Pakistan rather than West Pakistan due to the geographical distance. Historical, anthropological and literary narratives say that these people helped the Pakistani military to initiate genocide and mass rape against the Bengali community in 1971 (Schendel 2009; Ibrahim 2017; Anam 2007). So, when the war was over, they became targets of Bengali nationalists in Bangladesh. Though all of these non-Bengali migrants were not from Bihar, they were generally tagged as Biharis.

They faced counter-genocide, and the survivors live a terrible life without national identity in different camps (Schendel 2009, 173). Women became vulnerable targets of rape. Many were killed, and their breasts were cut with a special knife (Ranjan 2016, 5). Sarmila Bose has included many such instances of genocide and rape faced by the Bihari community in post-1971 Bangladesh.

During the war, Bihari migrants in Khulna (a city in Bangladesh) worked in jute mills, and they were massacred in large numbers in 1972. Bose estimates the number to be between 20,000 and 25,000, whereas the Bengali workers in those jute mills acknowledged that hundreds of Biharis were killed by Bengali people (2011a, 159). She writes, 'Men, women, and children were shot, knifed-killed in any way possible. The bodies were thrown into the river' (81). Bose describes another incident of Bihari people facing genocide in a railway colony in Shantahar in the Bangladeshi division of Rajshahi. According to a white paper by the Government of Pakistan, 15,000 people were killed in the massacre (85). Bose writes of Captain Sarwar of Pakistan who claimed that a massacre of Bihari rail workers and their families took place. According to Sarwar, as narrated by Bose, he and his colleagues saw horrible scenes in a pond and a nearby area that were full of dead bodies—men, women, and children—with evidence of grotesque bestiality such as infants stuck on spears and women's bodies slashed. Pakistani officials claimed that they had heard of such a massacre of the Bihari people, but nothing appeared in any media unlike the news of the genocide against Bengalis (85).

Born and brought up in a Bengali home, Bose had an added advantage in this research. She could interview the Bangladeshi people and read the sources related to the 1971 war in the vernacular. Bose claims that her book is the only evidence-based book on the 1971 war and considered it as unique as Sisson and Rose's book (1992). After more than thirty years of independence, Bangladesh has failed to provide academia with authentic, well-researched and scholarly evidence on the genocide, the rape and the victimisation (Bose 2011a, 5–6).

Bose presents the narratives in chronological order with a timespan between January 1971 and March 1972. Her work compiles the narratives of eyewitnesses from several areas of Bangladesh including Jessore (Jashore), Khulna, Mymensingh, Tangail, Rajshahi, Saidpur, Thakurgaon and so on. Sarmila Bose claims that the number of deaths and rapes mentioned in Bangladeshi narratives is a fabrication by the ruling government. She mainly accuses the Awami League[2] of such fabrication, and according to her, the Awami League has made the actual death toll ten times larger (46). While the media in Bangladesh and abroad claimed that a huge number of deaths had occurred during Operation Searchlight on 25 and 26 March, Bose uses the narratives of a few eyewitnesses of the incident to conclude that the number of deaths ranged between forty-four and seventy-three (66). She even cites Meghna Guhathakurta, the daughter of a Bengali intellectual and professor at the University of Dhaka, Jyotirmoy Guhathakurta, as saying that the number of casualties was 300 (67). Sarmila Bose presents the account of a Hindu man named Amiya Sur who claimed that in Shakharibazar Dhaka, there were fourteen to sixteen bodies. Anthony Mascarenhas's account states that the Pakistani army killed 8,000 Hindus in Shakharibazar Dhaka, but Bose's book maintains that most of the people in that region remained unharmed (75). Bose is also sceptical of Pakistan's representation of the victimisation of non-Bengali people in Bangladesh after the end of the war. The white paper by the government of Pakistan claims that 100,000 non-Bengali people were massacred by Bengali nationalists after the war. Bose thought that the figure was exaggerated just as Bangladeshi deeds exaggerated the number of Bengali people killed by the Pakistani army (180).

Bose points out that scholarly intervention in the 1971 war through the lens of women is yet to be developed. She praises Yasmin Saikia's attempt to document the narratives of victims and perpetrators regardless of their ethnic identity (Bose 2011a, 198). Many Bangladeshi and Indian critics accuse Bose of downplaying the aspect of rape as a war crime. Undoubtedly, based on the testimonies of Pakistani army officials, Bose refers to the rape incidents as 'opportunistic rape' (2007, 3864–3870). At the same time, she directly criticises the sexual assaults on non-Bengali women by Bengali nationalists as a part of ethnic cleansing (3870). She cites Ibrahim to claim that Bengali women, in most cases, were raped by Bengali men before being handed over to the Pakistani army. Hence, they would have been tagged as rape victims even if the Pakistani army had spared them (3870). She emphasises that the rape victims need to be interviewed by international scholars to maintain credibility (3871). She writes, 'Fiction cannot substitute for fact and every distraction from the true cases of rape takes us further away from discovering the nature of sexual violence in 1971 and compounds the injustice against the real victims, whose voices are still mostly silent' (3871). One of the reasons why Bose faced so much criticism not only from Bangladeshi people but also from international scholars is her seemingly biased representation of narratives. In many instances, she emulates Pakistani army personnel in calling the rapes of Bangladeshi women opportunistic wartime rapes, but, at the same time, appears to be highly critical when she mentions the incidents of non-Bengali rape victims based on the narratives of the survivors (Bose 2007, 2011a). She writes:

> Many of the non-Bengali victims appear to have been killed after sexual brutalisation by Bengali mobs as part of the 'ethnic cleansing' set off by the militant Bengali nationalist movement—as evidenced by the state of their corpses, while those who survived had no place in the 'heroine' category in independent Bangladesh. (Bose 2007, 3870)

In *Women, War, and the Making of Bangladesh: Remembering 1971*, Yasmin Saikia broadly focuses on the victimisation of the Bihari community, in general, and the gendered violence imposed on Bihari women, in particular, both by Bengali nationalists during the 1971 Liberation War and in its aftermath (2011b). The Bihari community became a soft target for the Bengali nationalists because they shared a common ethnic connection, speaking Urdu, with Pakistanis, and they were easily accessible in the urban or city areas where they worked in different factories and companies owned by the west Pakistani government (Saikia 2011b, 40–41). The Biharis were turned into a group of stateless refugees neither accepted by the independent Bangladeshi government nor by the separated Pakistani government. Saikia claims that more than 250,000 stateless Biharis still live in Bangladesh without basic human rights after they became confined to different camps like the Geneva Camp in Dhaka after the end of the 1971 war (41).

Saikia's narratives dismiss the claims of previous authors who changed the names of the victims because public exposure might bring more social stigmatisation. Saikia's narratives identify victims like Beauty, who faces multidimensional discrimination, for being the war baby of a single mother and for belonging to the Bihari community in Bangladesh. Beauty wants her story to be explored by the world because she is tired of invisibility (Saikia 2011b, 83). Beauty's mother is an acknowledged Birangona who was violated by Pakistani perpetrators during the 1971 war, but her marriage to a Bihari man after the war brought her more hatred from her fellow citizens. Beauty emerges as the epitome of survival after gendered violence and ethnic clashes. Saikia's narratives not only talk of sexual violence against women but also endeavour to point out the different roles of women as 'soldiers, social workers, caregivers, service providers, and other related tasks during the war' (88). To explore the multifaceted roles of women that went unacknowledged for decades, Saikia has emphasised oral history because traditional historiography may distort the truth (88–89).

Saikia shows how women have remained victims of war and counter-war during the war resolution process irrespective of their religion and ethnicity. A major portion of Saikia's book talks about the victimisation of Bihari women by Bengali nationalists who were acting on the accusations that the Bihari people collaborated with the

Pakistanis during the war. Chapter 3 of Saikia's book, titled 'Victims' Memories', has the testimonies of five rape victims that came to light for the first time in history. The first testimony is that of Nurjahan Begum, who lost all the male members of her family, including her five sons, brothers and nephews, in the ethnic clash between Biharis and Bengalis after the end of the Liberation War (Saikia 2011b, 153). She could save only a young son and a daughter in that ethnic conflict that went unrecorded in history, and she could hardly tell who the perpetrators had been in this incident. Nurjahan's sons and brothers were killed mercilessly in front of her: 'There was a river of blood and slaughtered heads of people were strewn all over' (154). Though Bihari men were primarily targeted, Bihari women were also not spared, as shown in Saikia's book. Many women were raped, and most were killed mercilessly (155). Through the voice of Nurjahan, Saikia has brought out the bitter truth of a war history that only focuses on the external struggle. The internal struggle, endured mostly by women, remains untouched and unfocused:

> When a war takes place, people write only about the external story, nobody wants to know and hear about the internal, intimate stories. Even today no one has written about it. It was not only Bengali women who were tortured. Everyone was looted and tortured during that time. Both Bengali and Bihari women were dehumanised. You should write about that. (Saikia 2011b, 155)

The experience of Bihari women stranded in the Geneva Camp in Bangladesh shows how women's lives are decided by their male counterparts and the policy makers of the society. Women did not primarily have any connection with the ethnic conflict between the Bengali-speaking and the Urdu-speaking community, but they were the ones who suffered the worst. The testimony of a Bihari woman named Khairum, who came from Kolkata to Bangladesh after her marriage not by her choice but out of compulsion, shows women's domestic as well as political subjugation. She did not have any choice in her migration. After the war, Bengalis wanted them to leave Bangladesh, but not even the Pakistani Government was ready to accept them (154). Khairum laments: 'Women are like cattle. They pack us off with the men as if we belong to a herd to be sent off for slaughter. My husband thought that our lives will be better in Pakistan. Hence, we left our homeland and came here' (154).

Recent academic work shows evidence of the victimisation of Bihari people, particularly Bihari women, in Bangladesh, especially after the end of the 1971 war. Bose's work is not from a feminist point of view. Women's issues, their stories and their agency do not feature in her narratives. Instead, they appear as victims. She does not conduct a sincere observation of their lives like Ibrahim, Mookherjee and Saikia did in their ethnographic intervention. The accounts of male eyewitnesses and Pakistani army officials form a major portion of her narratives. So, her ethnographic works on the women of the 1971 war can be assumed to be less connected to reality because women's narratives are hardly present in Bose's work. She takes a post-structural approach to ethnography for reframing the history of South Asia, especially the history of the Bangladesh 1971 war. Bose is very critical of the numbers rather than the narratives of the survival of women. In a typical manner, at the end of the book she compares the victims of the 1971 war with the Jewish victims of the Holocaust. Chaity Das writes,

> Bose is unable to see beyond numbers and almost characterises memories of the war in Bangladesh as a search for its own six million victims. One wonders what 'benefit' would accrue to the survivors and witnesses from comparisons with the fate of Jews in Hitler's Germany. (2013, 138)

Richardson's two important matrixes to evaluate ethnography, 'substantive contribution' and 'reflexivity', are apparent in Bose's ethnography (2000). Bose's work is substantive for two reasons. Many examples of non-Bengali Bihari people's experiences with genocide and rape in Bangladesh that were acknowledged and supported by writers such as Saikia (2011b), Ranjan (2016), Ara (2015) and so on are present in the book. Another contribution is her dealing with facts and fabrication regarding the data of deaths and rape victims of Bangladesh. Bose's work is also reflexive because she was very aware of the 1971 war since her childhood and grew up listening to the embedded narrative of the same war. Bose was in Kolkata when the war broke out, and she used to hear about the crisis of East Bengal's refugees in the Indian state of West Bengal from her family members. Her whole family was engaged in the rehabilitation process. Her father served as a paediatrician in the field hospital near the border, and her brother also used to go there. Her mother did relief work among the refugees (Bose 2011a, 1). Richardson's most crucial matrix for evaluating ethnography is the ethnography's connection to the truth: in his language, 'express reality' (2000). Bose appears to be the most controversial ethnographer among those featured in this research because of her theory of facts and fabrication. However, there is also strong support for her, despite her being accused of fabrication, from a few scholars and academicians of Bangladesh. In many cases, Bose undoubtedly downplayed the sacrifice of Bengali people, especially women, by aligning with Pakistan's narratives, but her claims about the inauthenticity of the death toll and the number of raped women are not baseless. Supporting Bose's assertion about the lack of empirical evidence about the martyrs and raped women of the 1971 war, Rubaiyat Hossain, an internationally acclaimed Bangladeshi filmmaker and scholar, writes in her blog:

> We surely have not done enough of systematic historical record-keeping of Muktijuddho history. The attempt to collect and compile Muktijuddho history has been fragmented and interrupted.... A very worthwhile document came out of this project, the fifteen volumes of Bangladesher Swadhinota Juddho Dolil Potro.... After a long interruption, in 1996, another project was undertaken by Mukitjuddho Gobeshona Kendra to collect oral history of Muktijuddho. However, after collecting 25,000 interviews in 19 compiled volumes this project

> was interrupted … there is no official figure based on empirical evidence of how many people actually died during the nine months of 1971. How many women were raped and how many war babies were adopted by foreign families still remain unknown. (2011)

Bose has been accused several times of attempting to deny the mass rape and genocide of 1971 by citing the narratives of Pakistani officials and Bangladeshi witnesses. Bose's interpretation of the number of victims did not go beyond the narratives of her Pakistani interlocutors who, since the end of the war, have dismissed the mass killing and rape (Ahsan 2012, 506). Saikia maintains a balance while documenting history with oral narratives. She displays professionalism and objectivity, empathising with not only the Bengali rape victims and their surviving war babies but also 'the Bihari or Urdu-speaking women who, in newly free Bangladesh, went through their own ordeals as the process of retribution got underway' (507). Saikia's scholarship, which revives women's voices in oral history in her ethnographic non-fiction, is discussed in the next section.

Women of the Unknown Register

Since the beginning of civilisation, women's situations, their engagement as fighters and their agency in wars and war resolution processes have been neglected by the main course of historiography. Though women have continued to contribute to the conflicts as armed fighters, nurses, volunteer workers and policy makers, history has failed to recognise that women have positive agency in the war (Cook 2006; Kaufman 2016). The greatest shortcoming of the historiography of Bangladesh is also the omission of women's positive contribution to the 1971 war (Amin et al. 2016). In the 1971 war, women suffered and showed unending courage during/after the war. Their plights are not always dependent on the ethnic politics between Bengali-speaking Bangladeshis and Urdu-speaking Pakistanis. They are more victims of their sexual identity, leading to both Bengali and Bihari communities facing violence and discrimination. In *Women, War, and the Making of Bangladesh: Remembering 1971*, Saikia shows how many women were victimised and many courageous women were forcefully marginalised despite their desire to fight for the nation (2011b). Saikia's accounts are not dimensional unlike most of the narratives of the Liberation War of Bangladesh. She portrays Bengali victims and Bihari victims on the same scale and shows that women of both communities suffered and remained unrecognised. In her ethnographic non-fiction, Saikia records the accounts of a few women who belong to an unknown category, neither Bengali victims or Bihari victims, and suggests that they be included as women of unknown register (2011b, 159).

The women of the 1971 war belonged to the subaltern position according to the definition of the term by Spivak (Cock 1992) because they had hardly any connection to the cultural sphere of mainstream Bangladesh. Over time, they have been forgotten, bypassed and silenced not only by patriarchy but also by the recent development of pro-religious sentiments over the spirit of the 1971 war in Bangladesh. Three decades after the war, in 2001, Saikia did her ethnographic intervention about the plight of women (of both Bengali and Bihari ethnicity) who faced the 1971 war in Bangladesh. The major problem addressed in her ethnographic research was the brooding silence in the lives of the survivors who have been forced to stay aside or live silently by society (Saikia 2011b, 109). She journeyed from Dhaka to Rangpur, a town in northern Bangladesh, and found women like Beauty who were willing to speak of their experience in the war (110).

In Saikia's narratives, the only woman connected to the 1971 war who overcame her subaltern position is Ferdousi Priyabhashini. Priyabhashini was the first rape survivor of the 1971 war who made her experience public, defying all taboos and ostracisation in post-war Bangladesh. She was hailed globally for her courage, and many international media outlets covered her story and documented her life in literature and films. However, breaking the silence in a country like Bangladesh where rape survivors face social ostracisation and even talk of rape is considered to be taboo was not an easy task (Saikia 2011b, 122). Ferdousi Priyabhashini's story proves that once a victim dares to break the silence, her courage is rewarded. Saikia mentions Ferdousi's present status in Bangladesh: 'In Bangladesh, every discussion about sexual violence in 1971 includes a mention of Ferdousi's experience. As such, Ferdousi has become an emblematic figure; this creates several problems in accessing her as an individual person' (122). Ferdousi's story is very special because it provides us with an insight into the gender violence in the war. She also locates herself within the larger context of gender violence in Bangladesh before and after independence. Ferdousi's victimhood may seem fictional to many scholars, and academicians like Sarmila Bose suspect fabrication in her story (125). However, Ferdousi defended her position to every possible extent in her interview. She is despised by many Bangladeshis because of her public revelation of the truth about rape. Her story reminds Bangladesh to accept the narratives as their own (125).

Ferdousi begins her story with the violence faced by her mother under the patriarchal control of her professor father to exemplify how gender violence is embedded in the social structure of South Asia where even women from aristocratic families are not spared. The body of a woman is used as a machine to tolerate patriarchal torture and produce babies. Ferdousi's mother had to endure abuse and produce a baby every year, resulting in Ferdousi having a total of eight siblings (Saikia 2011b, 127–129). Ferdousi's married life was equally unhappy. She had to work and maintain her family on her own because her husband was unemployed. She focuses on how she was violated many times by her countrymen who took advantage of her helplessness and poverty even before the war. She had lost all her love for the nation because she was struggling to maintain her family, three children and her unemployed husband. When the war broke out, she became the victim of the ethnic hatred of Pakistani soldiers who considered Hindu women targets of rape and abuse. Five men from the Pakistani military gang-raped her and left her in a bunker where she saw many women suffering agony in a very unhealthy ambience (134). Ferdousi was falsely charged with murdering a Pakistani, and the soldiers tried to make her confess through rape and torture. One man from the Pakistani army helped her escape her deplorable situation. His name was Altaf Kareem, with whom she fell in love. After the war ended, her story of rape and love affair with a rapist was unacceptable to her country's people. She was considered the 'number one' prostitute in free Bangladesh (135). So, coming out with the story of rape in a conservative society like Bangladesh has never been easy, but Ferdousi dared to break the mould and moved forward to prove that rape is not a matter of shame for the victim but shows the cowardliness of the rapists. She took almost twenty years to gain the courage to go public with her story of rape, and it was documented in 1999 for the first time in a magazine named *Bichitra* (135). In the article, Ferdousi regrets the condition of rape survivors like her in post-war Bangladesh. She tells the author, 'What I regret most is what happened to women after 1971.... We were physically assaulted in 1971, but after 1971 we were both physically and mentally assaulted' (136). Another reason why she is hated in Bangladesh is her frank acknowledgement of her love for a Pakistani rapist named Altaf Kareem. This kind of love of a victim for her rapist is not new in the context of the 1971 war. Neelima Ibrahim also records an incident in which a woman fell in love with a rapist and migrated to Pakistan to escape shame in her society (2017). So, whenever Ferdousi is interviewed by any media personnel in Bangladesh, she has to give an incomplete story of her survival because no one likes to listen to the story of her love for Altaf. For the first time, in her interview with Saikia, she was able to tell her complete story (Saikia 2011b, 136).

The last narrative in Chapter 3 is of Taslima's mother, a lady living in an infamous rural area of the Bangladeshi district of Dinajpur. Saikia retrieved the story of the victimisation of the Bihari community from the oral history of the common people in Dinajpur who acknowledged that the Pakistani army victimised Bengali people and, in return, the Bengali people assisted the Muktibahini to inflict violence on the Bihari community (Saikia 2011b, 137). Taslima's mother recorded her story in a diary, but unfortunately, she lost it. She had been waiting for decades with the hope that someday someone would come to document her story of survival and prejudices. Women like Taslima's mother were never featured in the official historiography of the Liberation War of Bangladesh, and their stories have remained untold because of the lack of proper documentation.

Chapters 3, 4 and 5 in Saikia's book contain the heart of women's narratives and describe the multifaceted experiences of the women in the 1971 war. These narratives form the main focus of this present chapter. The fictional portrayal of women's agency in the 1971 war has been discussed in the third chapter of this book. Here, women's agency and their stories of courage will be discussed through Saikia's feminist ethnographic intervention. Saikia has shown through women's narratives that the contribution of women in Bangladesh has gone largely unnoticed in the national register (2011b, 159). Accomplishing an ethnographic project on the lives of rape survivors of the 1971 war was difficult. During her fieldwork in Bangladesh, she was consistently discouraged from intervening in the lives of these women to avoid ostracisation from society (160).

The fourth chapter of Saikia's book comprises the accounts of three women who showed unusual courage during the tough time of Bangladesh's freedom struggle. The first narrative is of Suhasini Devi who was actively engaged in the rehabilitation of women after the 1971 war. She is from Sylhet, a division headquarters of Bangladesh, and is well known to the politicians and common people of the city for her humanitarian work. Her involvement in politics started much before the 1971 war. During the freedom struggle of India, she was a great follower of Gandhi and received direct guidance from the Mahatma

(Saikia 2011b, 160). Married at the age of twenty and widowed at the age of twenty-one, she was a true Gandhian visionary who sacrificed every moment as well as wealth for the sake of the people. Through Suhasini Devi's oral history, Saikia retrieved many stories of rape and war babies in the war. She delivered many war babies in her house after the war (162). In her conversation with Saikia, she is very frank about the prevailing public secrecy in Bangladesh about the rape and violation of women's bodies during the war. She acknowledges that one of her relatives was also raped, but she could not arrange a meeting with her because public exposure would ruin the peace of her personal life (162). Suhasini Devi appears to be very critical of the post-war crisis of women in Bangladesh. According to her, Bangladesh is governed by a female leader, but the women in Bangladesh do not enjoy the same privilege as their men even though they suffered a lot to free Bangladesh (163). About women's service in the war, she says, 'I think all women are brave. They need to have exposure to show their worth and stand up for the truth' (166).

The second narrative of a courageous woman in this chapter is of Dr Syed Ahmed Nurjahan from Chittagong, the second-largest city in Bangladesh. Dr Nurjahan worked on the abortion of war babies and the rehabilitation of survivors of sexual violence after the independence of Bangladesh. Her account discloses many hidden truths in the lives of the Birangona in post-war Bangladesh. She traced out the political reasons behind the mass abortion process that was conducted without concern for the physical and mental well-being of the women. She states, 'Abortion was introduced as a quick and certain measure to cleanse the odious Pakistani presence from the midst of Bangladeshi society' (Saikia 2011b, 168). She devoted herself to the job of abortion without being very concerned about its political implications. She helped many women to recover from the trauma of abortion and criticised the government's neglect of women's agency and their act of turning them into despicable bodies (169–170). She narrates her life story and her journey as a medical student from Dhaka Medical

College Hospital who went to England and finally joined Presidency General Hospital (PG Hospital, now known as Bangabandhu Sheikh Mujib Medical University Hospital) in Dhaka as an assistant professor when the war started (172). The war took from her the lives of her father and brother, and her mother was violated. So it was not an easy task for her to explain that traumatic memory to an ethnographer. A major portion of her narrative deals with the victimisation of her mother and her suffering as a rape survivor in Bangladesh. After the war, her main duty was abortion. She had to perform 200 abortion cases in a single day (174). Nurjahan says that most of the pregnancies happened before/after Bangladesh's freedom on 16 December, and the women who came for abortion were mostly Bengali between the age of eighteen and twenty-five years (174). Those women had many stories to tell, but Nurjahan was so preoccupied with the grief of her family tragedy that she was totally disinterested in their stories (174–175). She refers to a few other unknown stories of victimisation of Bihari women by Bangladeshi nationalists and Bengali women by the Indian Army, but she acknowledges that the number and the intensity of torture perpetrated by Pakistanis were the worst (175).

The story of Jharna Chowdhury from Noakhali, a district of Bangladesh, is exceptional in the sense that she was an activist who saved the lives of many children during the freedom struggle of Bangladesh. While bringing Jharna Chowdhury's narratives into focus, Saikia refers to the importance of oral history to reframe history because '[one] of the advantages of oral history is the unpredictability of where one can find evidence' (2011b, 177). Chowdhury was involved in looking after children in Gandhi Ashrama, an institution for orphaned children in Noakhali. They had to leave the Ashrama once the war started. Another major threat for them was that she was Hindu, and there were many Hindus among the children. With the help of an Indian minister, Jharna Chowdhury left Bangladesh for India so that she could keep her children safe during the struggle. She then saw the vast arrangement for training in Tripura, India, where many young Bengali girls used to work as volunteers (182–183). Chowdhury mentions how Indira Gandhi helped to liberate Bangladesh and how she personally came to know about Jharna Chowdhury's humanitarian work for the children (183). When she returned to Bangladesh, she had already become a centre of attraction for national and international visitors. Her narrative provides us with some instances of the fanaticism in Bangladesh in the name of war. When the interview took place, three decades had passed after the war, and Chowdhury wished that people's wounds from the tumultuous time of the 1971 war would heal.

The fifth chapter puts women's vital agency in the 1971 war directly into words. The social structure in Bangladesh and the prevailing patriarchal and religious orthodoxy made women's agency negligible in war and nation making. Hence, 'women's reality as secondary citizens limited the exercise of their agency even before independent Bangladesh was born' (Saikia 2011b, 187). The evidence in the second chapter of this book shows that women's agency in the 1971 war has been neglected in the main course of the historiography of Bangladesh, and they have been merely counted as victims of war in a few places. Despite women's praiseworthy contributions as survivors and fighters, they have never come up to the position of male *Muktijoddha*s in Bangladesh. Hence, women's agency has always been bypassed, and the stories of women's courage, like that of Laila's, never came up in history. Laila, the central figure of the first narrative in this chapter, showed unending courage during the war as per her claim. She was trained as an armed fighter in a biased, prejudiced and discriminatory ambience dominated by male authority (189). Laila was a medical student in Rajshahi, a divisional city in Bangladesh, when the war broke out, and she had to hide in different places because women of her age were special targets of the Pakistani army. Laila says that mothers in Bangladesh were trying to protect their young girls because everyone knew that Pakistani soldiers would not spare the young girls (192). When Laila was in hiding, her father was taken away by the Pakistani army. She could see his half-dead body from her hiding place, muttering and groaning in pain, but could not go near him out of fear (193). After her father's death, Laila moved to an island border town, Kustia, where she moved into her grandfather's house for safety. She describes the rape incident of a middle-class girl who was abandoned bleeding after the violation (195). With the help of her maternal uncle, Laila moved to Nadia in India with many other refugees. During that time, the government-in-exile of Bangladesh was formed in Kolkata under the leadership of Tajuddin Ahmed,[3] and Bengalis were being trained as *Muktijoddha*s and medical professionals (196–197). Being a medical student, Laila was asked to join the medical team to serve the wounded soldiers in the war. She was offered a decent salary, but she refused because she desired to fight from the front lines as a freedom fighter (198). She had to move a long way, and she walked all the way because she had no money to survive. Her legs became swollen, and she developed a kidney infection (198). At last, she was selected to be trained in the Gobra Camp, a camp mainly for female freedom fighters that operated from India under the supervision of the Bangladesh government-in-exile. Most of the girls in the camp were active in student politics before joining the camp, and they had managed, like Laila, to come there from different places in Bangladesh like Dhaka and Chittagong to join the freedom movement (199). In the camp, they learnt not only to fight but also to create massive awareness in favour of East Pakistan. Different India-based organisations like Ramakrishna Mission and Saint John Ambulance cooperated with them in their jobs (199). Girls were being sent to Agartala Camp as freedom fighters and medical professionals. Gobra Camp was recognised by the Bangladesh government as a female freedom fighters' training camp (200). Laila did not get a chance to carry out any assignments because before she completed training, Bangladesh was already free. She then moved to Bangladesh again to join the medical college (200). She worked to uplift women in post-war Bangladesh by spreading awareness about diseases, pregnancies and hygiene issues. Laila is very grateful to the spirit of the Liberation War of Bangladesh as it freed women from the bondage of domesticity (202). At the same time, she became highly critical of the failure of Bangladesh to recognise women's services in the war. Though their voices are being recorded gradually, the country had already lost many war heroines who have gone unnoticed or already died (202).

Women in Bangladesh played a great role in contemporary student politics across the country during the upheaval of the Bengali nationalist movement as elaborated in historical (Schendel 2009) and literary (Ara 2015) narratives. The narrative of Mumtaz Begum from chapter 5 of Saikia's book exemplifies women's engagement in the 1971 war. In 1971, Mumtaz was a leader of the Students' League, the students' union of the contemporary majority party Awami League. A daughter of a police inspector, Mumtaz was only twenty years old when she, along with her brother and sister, joined the Students' League in Jessore, her hometown (Saikia 2011b, 204). Like Laila, Mumtaz was very passionate about joining the freedom struggle, and hence, she moved to India to join the training. Being a girl, she did not get help and recommendations from higher authorities for training and accommodation. So, she had to stay in her grandfather's house in Kolkata where she was supported by the local Forward Bloc[4] member. The Gobra Camp in India did not much help Mumtaz's ambition because she did not want to be a nurse to the soldiers but a frontline fighter like male freedom fighters (207). She returned to Bogra, Bangladesh, after receiving her training and formed a camp of female fighters there with help from the administrator (207). However, she and her comrades struggled because they were not given the weapons that they had asked for. They joined a camp operated by the Border Security Force of India but were continuously discriminated against because they were girls (207). She was continuously interrogated and sometimes suspected of being a Naxal because a woman was not supposed to be involved in the freedom struggle. After settling in free Bangladesh, she and her activist associates suffered from an identity crisis because no one was there to recognise their activities for the country. She laments, 'Till today, we have not been recognised for the work we did during the liberation struggle. We had to prepare for the eventuality' (209). Even after the freedom struggle, they carried on their social work in Bangladesh. Unlike others, they did not surrender their weapons because they had many enemies who would have killed them (210). Later she was arrested and imprisoned for five years when one of her companions disclosed their secrets. Mumtaz reminisces about her days in student politics and the freedom struggle to show the readers how women faced discrimination because of their gender and not because of their ability. When the other students were given rifles for fighting, she only got a gun because women were not supposed to operate weapons like rifles (211). They starved and struggled but failed to get proper recognition for their service to the country. While women's services are not counted in official historiography, Mumtaz's oral history says that in a small town like Jessore alone, thirty girls fought directly in the war (212). Mumtaz's oral narrative provides vital instances of women's positive agency in the Liberation War of Bangladesh.

According to Richardson, one of the five matrixes of evaluating ethnography is to determine whether it is a substantive contribution or not (2000). Saikia's work truly is a worthwhile substantive contribution because it is a true ethnographic study conducted by the author in Bangladesh to learn about the plight of the women of the 1971 war. Feminist ethnography as a methodology of research is conducted over time. The research is initiated from a commitment to women to study gender issues across society (Aune 2009, 309). Saikia helped the Bengali and Bihari women living in Bangladesh to recall their memories through positive gestures and sincere engagement. Her direct engagement with the lives of women of the 1971 war makes her work a true feminist ethnographic work. When Saikia was conducting her ethnographic intervention among the female survivors of the war, she had to face many hurdles. The first problem was that people were disinterested in the survivors, who were marginalised in society (Saikia 2011b, 138). Locating the survivors was troublesome because 'women in Bangladesh who suffered the heinous crime of rape during the war have been forced to live with guilt and in silence for the rest of their lives' (140). This kind of silence in the lives of the victims of the 1971 war is also apparent in Mookherjee's book (2015b). Reflexivity is a matrix that evaluates an ethnographer's self-interest, self-awareness and self-exposure in that research (Richardson 2000). Saikia's reflexivity helped her to overcome all the obstacles associated with her mission, especially when she found that women were disinterested in talking to her because she had a male research collaborator. Saikia had a research associate named Rafi, and people interrogated her about her relationship with him. She told everyone that Rafi was her brother because it was not acceptable in rural Bangladesh for an unrelated man to accompany a woman. Women also hesitated to speak in front of Rafi, who stayed outside most of the time during the interview session (Saikia 2011b, 139). Saikia, like Spivak (1988), acknowledges that the survivors can speak up beyond every type of marginalisation if we can manage the time to listen to their stories (2011b, 140). The pervading silence in the lives of women forces ethnographers such as Saikia to think about why women should follow a life of suffering for a 'crime' that was not committed by them (141). Saikia's book is a groundbreaking work that brings out women's personal stories associated with the war of 1971. 'Saikia reminds us that woman's exclusion from nation-building narratives generates an incomplete understanding of conflicts and their aftermaths' (D'Costa 2012, 113). Saikia's book is probably the first of its kind to accommodate the oral history of valiant women such as Suhasini, Dr Nurjahan, Jharna Chowdhury, Laila Ahmed and Mumtaz Begum, who were not victims of the war but social workers, medical interns, armed fighters and caregivers. Such references to the valiant women of the 1971 war are absent in history but feature in recent creative non-fiction and fiction (Amin et al. 2016; Ara

2015; Anam 2007). Hence, apart from 'substantive contribution' and 'reflexivity', Saikia's feminist ethnographic works also 'express reality', another major matrix of evaluating ethnography as suggested by Richardson (2000).

Conclusion

The earlier discussion makes it clear that the traditional historiography of Bangladesh hardly pointed out feminist issues related to the war. Hence, a postmodern feminist intervention was inevitable to fill the gap. Neelima Ibrahim's book has remained a groundbreaking work in the feminist ethnographic reading of the 1971 war, but it slightly suffers from ethnic prejudices (2017). Forty years after the Liberation War of Bangladesh, feminist scholars such as Saikia (2011b) and Mookherjee (2015b) started to intervene in the matter and say that women have their own unique narratives connected to their memories to the war. Though Bose (2011a) faced many controversies for denying Bangladesh's claims connected to the number of rape victims, her book is important to us to know the condition of the Bihari people in general and Bihari women in particular in contemporary Bangladesh. Bina D'Costa's book is also noteworthy, but the authors have taken it as a secondary source for validating the truth in the other books (2011). While discussing the relevance of these books along with hers, Bina D'Costa writes:

> Drawing on multi-disciplinary research, respectively use the lenses of history, anthropology and international relations … [these writers] offer diverse perspectives, there is one essential and comparable standpoint. They place women's narratives at the core of retelling and redefining the meanings of 1971, questioning its truths, its memories, and its imaginations. (2012, 110)

A crosscheck of the narratives given earlier with a few other recent academic works on the 1971 war by Bangladeshi as well as international academicians will help to reassess the truth to an extent. Though the victimisation of the Bihari community through murder, rape and confinement got no place in the earlier narratives of Ibrahim and a few others, it became a major topic of discussion in later Bangladeshi narratives as well. Dilruba Z. Ara's fictional narrative *Blame* shows the parallel victimisation of the Bengali community by Pakistanis and the Bihari community by Bengali nationalists as revenge (2015). Ibrahim's book describes the ethnic struggle between the Bengali community and the Bihari community during the Liberation War of Bangladesh but takes one-sided positions to show the Biharis as perpetrators (2017, 114–119). Nayanika Mookherjee's narratives may be considered an extended version of Ibrahim's. In both books, the plight of the Birangona got priority in the contexts of the 1990s and 2010s respectively. While Ibrahim has limited her focus to the spectrum of the oral narratives of the Birangona, Mookherjee extends the scholarship into a triangulation of ethnography, state and human rights community, and the literary and visual representation of the rape survivors. Saikia has maintained a balance, switching her narratives between Bengali and Bihari victims of the 1971 genocide. However, Sarmila Bose's version of the truth has remained the most controversial and highly debatable. Dr Geoffrey Davis, a medical graduate from Sydney, was brought to Bangladesh by the United Nations to perform and monitor the abortions of war babies after the end of the war. He refuted Pakistan's claims of exaggeration and affirmed that the reported number of women raped by the Pakistani military is a conservative estimate compared to the actuality (D'Costa 2011, 197). Hence, Sarmila Bose's claims of exaggeration are not validated by those who voluntarily helped Bangladesh recover from its terrible state after the genocide. Nayanika Mookherjee also refuted Bose's claims of exaggeration and criticised her attempt to fabricate history. She says, 'To take Bose's word for it would be an unfortunate misreading' (Mookherjee 2011).

Despite the conflicts, one thing common to all these feminist ethnographic narratives is that they have pinpointed the tendency to suppress women's stories. Even in the traditional narratives of the war by Neelima Ibrahim and a few other memoirists, there is always an over-emphasis on the stories of Bengali rape victims, and the non-Bengali women do not find any mention. Modern post-conflict narratives of victims by Nayanika Mookherjee and Yasmin Saikia have hinted at unique issues such as the victimisation of non-Bengali Bihari women during the 1971 genocide. Their narratives engage in an in-depth analysis, which they managed within a very short period as a part of their research work. The narratives of Sarmila Bose appear to be one-sided and conflict with existing narratives of the 1971 genocide. Negotiating the spaces of truth or factual information is a doubtful trajectory even in narrative non-fiction of the genocide. Despite the best intentions to claim justice and truth in a post-conflict society, these narratives fail and falter but not without offering deep insights into past events that were otherwise disregarded.

Truth is a relative matter in the case of genocide, which also applies to the narrative non-fiction dealing with genocidal violence and rape in the 1971 war. Since the interviewers and memoirists relied on second-hand information in most cases, the scope of partial fabrication cannot be denied. In genocide, the truth disappears with its dead and is fabricated under the influence of a new set of ideologies. The conflicting narratives of the rape victims of the 1971 Liberation War of Bangladesh prove that we are yet to reach the truth. However, what is special to Bangladeshi ethnographers is their connections to the sociopolitical events of the country. Ibrahim was directly associated with the rehabilitation process of the rape victims. Bose's narrative lacks feminist scholarship because she has given more priority to the discrepancy in the numbers of victims and dead people in the war rather than the plights of victims and women fighters. Therefore, factual information can hardly be found even in the narrative non-fiction of the genocide, though narrative non-fiction is meant to bring the truth unconditionally Despite such limitations, these multidimensional narratives provide new insights into past events that had long been ignored. Narrative non-fiction makes marginalised voices public to claim justice and rights in a post-conflict society.

According to Richardson and Pierre, the actual blurring of the genre has made us understand that all writings are narrative (2018). Hence, the evaluation technique of a true fiction is different from that of a work of social science. The evaluation should not differ on whether the writing is fiction or non-fiction but should look into the matter of how the truth is claimed. Postmodernism permits the blurring of genres and theoretical lenses to evaluate the narratives of ethnographers, but at the same time, it raises doubts about the authenticity of the claims made by the ethnographers. Hence the truth always remains relative, and we only come to know some versions of it. The emergence of feminist ethnographic non-fiction presented several versions of truth related to the gender violence in the 1971 war. Though their connection to the ultimate truth is questionable, their approach to a multidimensional reading of the historiography of the 1971 war cannot be denied. With an evaluation of the narratives of Ibrahim (2017), Mookherjee (2015b), Bose (2011a) and Saikia (2011b) through Richardson's matrixes of evaluating ethnography (2000), it is clear that most of these feminist ethnographic non-fictional texts were grounded within the context of the 1971 war. The ethnographers were aware, interested and conscious of their study, and they reached closer to the truth. Their ethnographic literature opened up the research of the 1971 war to future academia to ensure more engagement with the issues. In the words of Richardson and Pierre, 'There is no such thing as "getting it right," only "getting it" differently contoured and nuanced. When using creative analytical practices, ethnographers learn about the topics and about themselves that which was unknowable and unimaginable using conventional analytical procedures, metaphors, and writing formats' (2018, 1415).

The postmodern feminist writings of the 1971 war by different ethnographers help us to access women's narratives of victimisation, their agency in the war and their post-war suffering in South Asia. The writers brought us the unknowable and unimaginable stories of women connected to the war with different methods of analysis, rhetoric and style. They have also opened up the scope to further elaborate and explore these issues in the same or different contexts.

Notes

1 'Joy Bangla' is a slogan used in Bangladesh since the 1971 freedom struggle, popularised by Sheikh Mujibur Rahman, the first prime minister of independent Bangladesh. It means 'victory to Bengal'.

2 The Awami League is a political party that was formed by Sheikh Mujibur Rahman during the upheaveal of Bengali nationalism in East Pakistan prior to the 1971 war. In 2022, it is the largest political party of Bangladesh, forming the ruling government.

3 Tajuddin Ahmed (1925–1975) was a leader and freedom fighter of Bangladesh. He was the first prime minister of Bangladesh's government-in-exile formed in India.

4 Forward Bloc is a political party that was formed by Netaji Subhas Chandra Bose in 1939 to involve the Indians in India's freedom movement.

5

Feminist Narratives of 1971: The Present and the Future

Rereading the Gendered History

Women's experiences in the 1971 war of Bangladesh have only received sporadic mentions in historical, literary and ethnographic narratives. So, a structural and systematic analysis is required. The Bangladesh Liberation War seems to be one of the most ambiguous conflicts in the history of South Asia for researchers and academicians due to the contesting/conflicting narratives, less historical evidence and the lack of scholarly articles. The 1971 war involved three South Asian nations. Though it was primarily an ethnic conflict between Bangladesh and Pakistan, India backed Bangladesh with arms and military aid to help it gain independence from Pakistan. Apart from the political and ethnic debate, the most important factor of the 1971 war is the number of casualties and rape victims. Bangladeshi narratives claim that more than 3,000,000 people were brutally killed, and 200,000 to 400,000 women were raped in the nine-month struggle (Sundar and Sundar 2014, 44; Linton 2010b, 194). On the other hand, Pakistani sources state that there were 26,000 deaths and negligible instances of rape (Linton 2010b, 194, 202). Due to the lack of proper evidence, the Bangladesh War of Independence was a popular research topic even three decades after the war. In the Bangladeshi historiography, the external conflicts between Pakistanis and Bangladeshis are apparent, but the inner conflict experienced by mostly women of Bihari and Bengali ethnicity in their domestic and social lives has remained untouched (Saikia 2004, 275). In 1993, the

International Crimes Tribunal was set up by the United Nations Court to seek international justice for rape and genocide, but surprisingly, the mass rape incidents of the 1971 war received hardly any mention there (Linton 2010a, 187). The gender issues of the war have remained almost untouched because the historical data is misleading, gendered and conflicting. The authenticity of the single-sided focus has been questioned several times by researchers such as Sarmila Bose (2011a), Amit Ranjan (2016) and Qasmi (2017). Ahmad points out that the field of humanities and social sciences faces trouble working on the Bangladesh Liberation War due to the lack of sound historical evidence and scholarly materials (2016). The critical element is the representation of women in the history of the 1971 war: they are rarely acknowledged as contributors to the freedom struggle of Bangladesh.

We have pointed out women's neglected roles in the historiography of the 1971 war by writers from Bangladesh (Rahman [1982] 2009; Iqbal 2008), Pakistan (Malik 2008) and India (Raghavan 2013). This book has been corroborated by the writings of a Western historian (Schendel 2009) to infer that neither South Asian historiography nor Western representation of the 1971 war has been able to portray women's stories, their role as fighters and their post-war plight. Ethnographic fiction and non-fiction have given flesh and blood to women's voices and rescued them from a subaltern position to become significant contributors to the making of history. Subalterns can speak for themselves only if they can bypass the politics of patriarchal representation (Spivak 1988). Feminist ethnography challenged the marginalisation and the tendency to avoid representation of women's experiences, and it sought to give a voice to the voiceless (Aune 2009, 310). Feminist ethnography helps feminist researchers foreground their knowledge based on 'lived experience' and 'concrete realities' of people's lives (Ghosh 2016, 2). We have studied fiction (Ara 2015; Anam 2007; Shamsie 2002), and non-fiction (Ibrahim 2017; Mookherjee 2015b; Bose 2011a; Saikia 2011b) that are mostly based on such lived experiences of the women of the 1971 war. Female anthropologists and writers, out of self-interest, tried to bring the stories of these women known through literature. Despite its role in restructuring historiography, ethnographic literature is not free from subjectivity and can occasionally be accused of fabrication. Hence, it needs a thorough evaluation to maintain objectivity. The literature available on the 1971 war mostly deals with the one-sided representation of gender and political issues. There is a lack of evaluation of existing ethnographic literature. 'We are in a new age where messy, uncertain multivoiced texts, cultural criticism, and new experimental works will become more common, as will more reflexive forms of fieldwork, analysis, and intertextual representation' (Denzin and Lincoln 2018, 60–61). This book combines all experimental works on the women of the 1971 war, compares intertextual representation and evaluates those works through the select lens of Richardson (2000).

Richardson and Pierre opine that postmodernism suspects all existing truths, but it does not deny anything (2018). Instead, it welcomes open and critical experimentation with new methods, which also come under critical evaluation. This book analyses gender issues of the 1971 war through the lens of feminist ethnographic fiction and non-fiction, and then it evaluates these narratives through the lens of Richardson's select matrixes of evaluating ethnography to highlight women's multifaceted experience in/after the war in Bangladesh. Though Richardson (2000) has provided five matrixes for evaluating ethnography, the postcolonial feminist lens has emphasised three factors to an extent—the context of the ethnography, the ethnographers' consciousness, and ethnography's connection to the truth. These are similar to three of Richardson's five criteria. Richardson's approach is truly postmodern. He has not imposed any hard and fast rules for such evaluation. Instead, he suggests, 'I believe it is our continuing task to create new criteria and new criteria for choosing criteria' (Richardson 2000, 254). The first chapter of this book discusses how postcolonial feminist ethnographers found substantive contribution, ethnographers' consciousness (reflexivity) and ethnography's connection to the truth (express reality) to be the most common and most important criteria for ethnographic work. Richardson's other two criteria have not been chosen for evaluation because the feminist ethnographic works of the 1971 war are very new to academia (2000). So, analysing how that literature influenced others to write on it is tough. Also, the researcher's feelings and connection to these ethnographic works have been avoided because this study has been done for purely academic purposes, avoiding subjectivity.

The patriarchal nature of history has been a matter of discussion not only in postcolonial times but also since the advent of modernist thoughts and ideas, much before feminism became organised thoughts and movements. Critical works, starting from those by Woolf ([1929] 1977) to those by modern feminists such as Spivak (1988) and Saikia (2011b), say that women's voices have been rendered invisible by the political and patriarchal representation of history. The sincere efforts of feminist writers and ethnographers have taken the voices of women beyond historical representation to shape traditional public consciousness about women's role in history. Women's self-narratives are important because our ideology and consciousness are shaped by the dominant cultural stories of gender, racial identity, sexual identity and so on (Lee 1997, 2). We have tried to reread the historiography of the Liberation War to trace the position of women there and found that women occupy a very negligible place in those books of history. The historiography of Bangladesh mostly depicts women as neglected and defiled victims in the war and hardly touches on their agency, struggle and post-war condition (Iqbal 2008; Rahman [1982] 2009). From Pakistan's perspective, history seems to be oblivious to the struggle the people of Bangladesh endure (Malik 2008). The scholarly approach from India also appears to fail in its portrayal of women's engagement in the war (Raghavan 2013). Instead, it typifies the patriarchal representation by showing the war as a fruit of external politics by the men. Praiseworthy attempts have been made by some authors like Schendel to incorporate women's stories into history, but that is also based on literary narratives rather than women's real-time experiences (2009). We analysed (in Chapter 3) how contemporary novels (Ara 2015; Anam 2007; Shamsie 2002) of South Asia have seriously dealt with the historical event of the 1971 war in Bangladesh and traced many women's issues such as their subjugation through blame, their agency in the war and their victimisation in the ethnic politics of their men. These novels are examples of feminist ethnographic novels because they deal with issues based on the novelists' real-time experiences with the women of the 1971 war. We have also taken a few non-fictional accounts of contemporary women ethnographers (in Chapter 4) for a detailed study of the lives of women who were not only victims but also social workers, healthcare professionals and fighters in the war and whose voices have been suppressed in post-conflict Bangladesh.

Feminist Narratives as 'Substantive Contribution'

The select feminist fictional works about the Liberation War of Bangladesh are substantive contributions as we see in these three novels that deal with three unique gender issues related to the war with a detailed and close observation of the lives of women in the 1971 war. Women's victimisation through social blaming is common in world history. Instead of getting justice, rape survivors are mostly blamed by their own people (Wakelin and Long 2003, 477). Dilruba Z. Ara's *Blame* describes the oppression of courageous women through blame in the context of the 1971 war (2015). The novel also deals with the journey of two rape victims, Laila and Gita, from being fighters to becoming victims and subsequently ostracised by society. When the main course of historiography has been silent about women's positive role in the 1971 war, Anam's female characters Rehana and Maya, in her novel *A Golden Age* (2007), exemplify women's involvement in social work during the war, like sheltering freedom fighters, helping refugees and providing medical services to wounded soldiers and homeless people. Shamsie's *Kartography* points out a completely untouched issue, the plight of migrated Bengali women in Pakistan and their continuing subjugation due to the ethnic politics of the 1971 war (2002).

By documenting the oral narratives of victims and activists, feminist ethnographic non-fiction has helped to explore a few more gender issues connected to the 1971 war that have been overlooked in history. The post-war condition of the Birangona, their ostracisation, their enforced migration and their physical and psychological trauma are major parts of the non-fictional accounts of Ibrahim (2017) and Mookherjee (2015b). Bihari women's mass victimisation in ethnic politics got a place in the writings of Bose (2011a), Saikia (2011b) and Mookherjee (2015b). Women's narratives of their participation in the 1971 war as fighters and social workers constitute the main portion of the ethnographic literature of Saikia (2011b).

'Reflexivity': The Writers' Connection to the 1971 War

All the feminist narratives, fiction and non-fiction, discussed here express the writers' ethnographic endeavour and their deep connection to the sociopolitical context of the Liberation War of Bangladesh. In the second chapter, two Bangladeshi diasporic novels and one Pakistani novel have been discussed. Dilruba Z. Ara, a Bangladeshi novelist based in Sweden, spent her earlier life in Bangladesh, and the novel *Blame* (2015) is the fruit of her experience with the war (Haque 2016). Reflexivity is obvious in Tahmima Anam's *A Golden Age* too (2007). Anam, being a professional anthropologist from Harvard, has been able to convert her ethnographic endeavour into fiction. She was raised in a family where her parents and grandmother helped her to recreate the memory of the 1971 war based on their own direct experiences with the war. Anam interviewed many freedom fighters and acknowledged those people who encouraged her to undertake the project of documenting women's agency in the 1971 war through her characters (2007, 276). Shamsie, despite being a part of the Pakistani diaspora, shares a bond with the people and demography in Karachi (2010). This reflexivity of these writers helped them to retrieve the experience of the women of the 1971 war.

The select non-fiction that constitutes the fourth chapter of this book also shows the reflexivity of ethnographers such as Ibrahim, Mookherjee, Bose and Saikia in documenting women's experiences in the war based on their oral narratives. Language becomes an important tool for ethnographers to make their works more credible. If the informants use the same language, the works become more credible (Muecke 1994). In this sense, the non-fictional narratives of Ibrahim (2017), Mookherjee (2015b) and Bose (2011a) appear to be credible because the authors belong to the same Bengali ethnicity and are aware of the sociocultural perspective of the informants. Ibrahim worked as a social worker during and after the 1971 war to rehabilitate the Birangona, and she saw their lives and suffering first-hand. Though Mookherjee was not an insider like Ibrahim, she undertook a praiseworthy ethnographic project to document the plight of the Birangona in 1990s Bangladesh when the country was going through extreme turmoil due to communal tension. Bose's reflexivity is connected to her consciousness of the 1971 war since her childhood. She was raised in a family in Kolkata where her parents were actively engaged in service for Bengali refugees who had migrated to India during the outbreak of the 1971 war (Bose 2011a, 1). Saikia was also an outsider like Mookherjee, but she, with the help of her research associate, travelled to every corner of Bangladesh to find women whose lives and their connection to the war had already been forgotten by the people of Bangladesh. Saikia's multidimensional research to retrieve women's engagement, their victimisation in ethnic politics and their positive agency in the war is the most balanced work about women's connection to the 1971 war in Bangladesh. Saikia has proved that the understanding of a conflict becomes incomplete if women are excluded from the context (D'Costa 2012, 113).

'Express Reality' and the Scope of Fabrication

The emergence of contemporary feminist ethnographic fiction and non-fiction has contributed to 'express reality' in/across the society of Bangladesh in different ways through familiarising the people with several gender issues that remained untouched in history and public consciousness. Historical representation says much about women's victimisation in the war, but their internal struggle and post-war plights have hardly been portrayed there (Rahman [1982] 2009; Iqbal 2008). We have focused on works of fiction and non-fiction that portray women's victimisation followed by their ostracisation in post-war Bangladesh. The proximity to the truth can be verified from other scholarly works and features in books, journals and newspapers. Recent feminist narratives of the 1971 war are relevant because they have revealed the multifaceted victimisation of women's bodies in ethnic conflicts. The use of women's bodies as a medium of patriarchal atrocities is not new to the 1971 war. The 1947 Partition also saw many instances. About 75,000 to 100,000 Hindu, Muslim and Sikh women were raped, mutilated and harassed by people of other communities during the Partition violence, 'a direct consequence of the appropriation of women's bodies for symbolic uses within the dialectics of patriarchal communalism' (Navarro-Tejero 2019, 44–45). Bangladesh experienced such severe gender violence in the 1971 war that it became a major point of discussion in Bangladeshi high culture and popular culture since the war. Recent scholarly ethnographic interventions have gradually exposed different angles of gender violence. Exploiting women's bodies for the sake of ethnic politics in the 1971 war is shown by Ara (2015), Ibrahim (2017), Mookherjee (2015b), Bose (2011a) and Saikia (2011b). In the 1971 war, rape was multidimensional. Bengali women, especially Hindu women, were special targets because the Pakistani army considered the Bengali people infidels (Ara 2015; Mookherjee 2015b). By raping the women, they wanted to degrade their spirit and morality to fight back. They also did not spare the Muslim women, and the number of rapes is supposed to be somewhere between two hundred thousand to three hundred thousand, according to the general representation of the history of Bangladesh (Linton 2010b). Though Bose has referred to such intensity of gender violence as 'opportunistic rape' by the military (Bose 2007), the narratives of Mookherjee (2015b) and Ibrahim (2017) say that strong ethnic politics played a role behind such gender violence. Mookherjee dismisses Bose's claims of fabrication and attempts to downplay the number of rapes (2011). Dr Davis's interview with Bina D'Costa also suggests that a large number of women were raped in the 1971 war (2011). Lisa Curtis adds to the criticism about the number of rape victims with her opinion that the violence and rapes perpetrated by the Pakistani military were far more than what people on the outside came to know (quoted in Boissoneault 2016).

The outcome of feminist ethnographic narratives has reformed the public consciousness in Bangladesh to an extent, and a major portion of Bangladeshi people have started to acknowledge the contribution of the Birangona and other fighters in the war. This book has unveiled women's agency in the 1971 war through their own narratives in fiction and non-fiction. Tahmima Anam's female activists Rehana and Maya in *A Golden Age* (2007), Dilruba Z. Ara's female freedom fighters Laila and Gita in *Blame* (2015) and Yasmin Saikia's healthcare professionals Laila and Nurjahan and fighters cum social activists Mumtaz, Suhasini and Jharna in *Women, War, and the Making of Bangladesh* (2011b) are all critical in reframing history and public consciousness, not only in Bangladesh but also in South Asia. The women who endured sexual violence, who were earlier considered the epitome of shame, have been gradually recognised not as defiled women but as the heroes of the war. Asma Akter Eka, the fifteen-year-old daughter of a rape survivor, unequivocally acknowledges that she is very proud of her mother and aunt for their sacrifice in the Liberation War of Bangladesh, both of whom were raped during the war (Das and Berning 2011). Women's narratives have helped Bangladeshi scholars and intellectuals to investigate the lives of women who were associated with the 1971 war and whose lives have continued in silence. The coverage of Bangladeshi media of Taramon Bibi is an example. Taramon Bibi was directly involved in the war in her village Shankar Madhabpur in Kurigram District of Bangladesh in Sector 11. The title 'Bir Pratik' was conferred on her for her bravery in the 1971 war. However, such women are yet to get recognition and other privileges accorded to the *Muktijoddha*s. The glory of being freedom fighters is still enjoyed by male fighters only in what seems to be the greatest failure of a South Asian country like Bangladesh in acknowledging their female fighters (Amin et al. 2016). Media coverage of Rama Chowdhury, a Birangona popularly known as *Ekattorer Janani* (the mother of 1971), highlighted her extreme struggle for life, livelihood and recognition till her death in 2018 (Huda 2018; Karim 2018). The recent media coverage pinpoints two vital issues: the indifference of Bangladesh to the sacrifices made by its war heroines and the growing consciousness of people about the female fighters of the war. The second issue is essential for the establishment of a secular and gender-neutral country to maintain the spirit of the 1971 war. The greatest achievement of the emergence of women's narratives is the trial of the war criminals of Bangladesh in recent times conducted by the Awami League government. In 2009, the International Crimes Tribunal was set up in Bangladesh for the legal trial of Razakars or pro-Pakistani people living in Bangladesh who committed genocide and gender violence in 1971. Till 2019, though it has delivered the verdicts of thirty war criminals, this trial faced much criticism for not having any international judges like other crime tribunals in Nuremberg, Tokyo,

Rwanda and Yugoslavia (Mollah 2019, 1). The testimonies of three girls were crucial in the successive tribunals of the war criminals in Bangladesh. As many of these accused war criminals were engaged in right-wing politics in Bangladesh, their supporters showed their rage with violent protests, referring to such trials as extrajudicial killings, and sought attention from international humanitarian organisations to prevent this. For instance, in 2013, sixty-five people lost their lives in mob protests and atrocities when Delawar Hossain Sayedee (a right-wing political leader) was sentenced to death by the tribunal (7). The narratives of victims play a major role in the recognition and final judgement of several war criminals. Despite protests from different sides and the ostracisation of women who testified in these trials, the process continued, and more alleged war criminals came under the tribunal's jurisdiction. In August 2018, five war criminals were sentenced to death by the tribunal, when six women 'who survived the abduction and rape came forward to testify during the trial' (Zwier 2018). Such an incident proves that women are gradually bypassing the politics of representation, establishing their voices in policy making and rereading the existing history of a country like Bangladesh.

Women's dislocation through migration amidst the ethnic conflict is another matter discussed in this book through the writings of Ibrahim (2017) and Shamsie (2002). Women migrated or many of them committed suicide after the end of the war to save themselves from ostracisation in post-war Bangladesh. Other evidence, like that of D'Costa (2011) and Das and Berning (2011), also supports such a representation of enforced migration and suicide in mass numbers in/after 1971 in Bangladesh. They refer to women who migrated after the war because they could hardly live in Bangladesh because of the shame and hatred inflicted upon them by their countrymen. They migrated to India and, sometimes, with their rapists to Pakistan for the sake of their survival.

Bihari women's victimisation in the 1971 war and the aftermath is another aspect that has been overlooked by the history of the war. Thanks to contemporary ethnographic interventions, this matter has come to light. Willem Schendel says that the Bihari people faced a similar counter-genocide at the end of the 1971 war (2009). Amit Ranjan cites Anthony Mascarenhas to give information about non-Bengali people (especially migrated Biharis) who also faced savagery during the war in Bangladesh (2016). Many women were raped, and their breasts were cut with special knives. The death toll of non-Bengali people may have been as high as 100,000 (Ranjan 2016, 5). Bihari people's statelessness and their victimisation in the ethnic politics in post-war Bangladesh are major issues discussed by Saikia (2011b) and Bose (2011a). Bose records the accounts of several stateless Bihari people who still live in different camps in Bangladesh. According to such narratives, the Biharis were killed mercilessly, and their women were raped and humiliated by violent mobs in Bangladesh. The media, however, ignored such reports (Bose 2011a, 81–85). Though Bose's main concern is the Bihari community in general, Yasmin Saikia looks into the lives of Bihari women in Bangladesh, in particular, to know the pain they endured since the end of the war (2011b). Saikia tells the stories of many Bihari women who migrated to East Pakistan with their husbands because they thought that in Pakistan, they would have a better life. However, they have been targets of the ethnic politics of their men, in which they have hardly any involvement (Saikia 2011b, 154). The claims of Bose (2011a) and Saikia (2011b) are not baseless as we see the emergence of Bihari victims in the writings of Bangladeshi academicians too. Haider, based on his interview with seventy-five Biharis in three Bihari camps across Bangladesh, states that Biharis are still deprived of citizenship and human rights in Bangladesh (2018). As the Bihari people lost their wealth after the 1971 war, many of their women are reduced to begging, and girls experience enforced child labour, child marriage and even prostitution for the sake of livelihood (35s). So, more intervention is needed to bring out the pitiful condition of Bihari women in Bangladesh and their continuous subjugation through the ethnic politics connected to the 1971 war.

The politics of representation only presented the Bihari community in Bangladesh as an enemy class who allegedly opposed Bangladeshi nationalism and sided with the Pakistani army to conduct genocide and rape. According to the narratives on every side, many of them undeniably collaborated with Pakistanis. The history of South Asia, however, hardly records the counter-genocide and gender violence inflicted on their people and their women as vengeance. After the emergence of women's ethnographic narratives like that of Bose (2011a) and Saikia (2011b), the people of Bangladesh have started to look at the Bihari community of Bangladesh through a humanitarian lens. They have started to acknowledge that as a minority community, they have the right to proper citizenship and other rights in Bangladesh. In 2008, the Supreme Court of Bangladesh granted citizenship to those Biharis who were minors during the 1971 war or were born after the war (Cecconi 2019). The citizenship issue of a huge number of refugees remained unresolved. The lives of women in the congested camps are terrible, and many of them become targets of sex trafficking at a very early age. Recently, several Bangladeshi scholars investigated the deplorable living conditions in the camps and the degraded condition of their women. Mohammad Kamrul Hasan Arif, a Bangladeshi scholar, writes that the tripartite agreement between Bangladesh, India and Pakistan could not settle the issue of citizenship of Bihari people, with more than 300,000 Bihari still living in different camps of Bangladesh and their issue of citizenship unclear (2015). Rock Ronald Rozario and Stephan Uttom from Bangladesh write that the Bangladeshi government has been generous in granting the Biharis citizenship since 2010, but they have been still living in inhuman conditions in different camps without basic human rights (2019). In the seventy camps across the country, women also become victims in several ways, like frequent clashes with the police. The Bangladeshi people have gradually started to feel solidarity with the Bihari people regarding their identity, basic rights, citizenship and women's rights, showing the positive side of humanity.

Feminist ethnographic narratives have helped to reconstruct Pakistani consciousness about the rape and genocide that were committed back in 1971 by their predecessors. The present generation of Pakistanis is not so oblivious to the bitter history of Pakistan. They acknowledge it with confessions of the crimes by their men. Kamila Shamsie, a Pakistani diasporic writer, is very critical of the oblivious nature of Pakistani narratives about the genocide and rape that happened in 1971. When she visited an exhibition about the 1971 war in London, she shared the contradiction in public consciousness regarding the atrocities that happened at the time.

> I turn to the Bangladeshi photographers in order to fix my gaze on that blood-soaked epoch. I don't even realise I'm doing this, at first. I think I'm looking at a man's head, cast in marble; the sculpture is cheek-down amid a cluster of stones, almost camouflaged by them. Then I read the caption: 'Dismembered head of an intellectual killed 14 December 1971 by local collaborators of Pakistani army. Bangladesh.' It is extraordinarily eerie, and sad. There are other pictures of that period, too. Many, if not all, will probably be familiar to anyone from Bangladesh; none are part of Pakistan's consciousness. (Herbert 2011, 159)

Uma Chakraborty, a contemporary feminist scholar, shares her experience at a conference in Lahore. She avers that female scholars from Pakistan do not suppress the gendered violence initiated by Pakistan in the 1971 war. They not only apologised to the Bangladeshi scholars for the rape and genocide but also claimed that Pakistani women had always raised their voices against such atrocities by their male counterparts (Roy 2019). Nowadays, the present generation of Pakistanis, including scholars, professors, diplomats and scientists, confess that their predecessors did much harm to the people of Bangladesh, and they ask for an unconditional apology to Bangladesh for it. They are especially critical of their people for the genocide and gender violence in Bangladesh. Pervez Hoodbhoy, a reputed nuclear physicist and defence analyst, says that under the misdirected vision of Muhammad Ali Jinnah, the founder of Pakistan, Pakistan wronged Bangladesh to an extent. He adds, 'His country has mistreated, exploited and massacred the Bangladeshi people in 1971' (Zaman 2020). A.U. Qasmi, a professor of history at the University of Lahore, confesses to a sense of guilt and locates the politics of representation of history in Pakistan as well as Bangladesh as he moves through the memories of war at the University of Dhaka (2017). Unlike the Indian author Bose, who claims that the number of rapes recorded is fabricated (2011a) and opportunistic (2007), Pakistani author Anam Zakaria acknowledges that due to the army dictatorship, the death toll is estimated to be three million with hundreds and thousands of raped women (2019). Such gestures and acknowledgement of the Pakistani people show the positive side of the emergence of feminist ethnographic narratives by global academicians that helped to break the silence and reframed the consciousness of Pakistan about the 1971 war.

Women's oral narratives of their own lives are not always neutral. Sometimes, they are embedded with the dominant gender stories (Lee 1997, 2). Hence, the ethnographic narratives in fiction and non-fiction also suffer from one-sidedness or prejudices because of the ethnographers' connection with the dominant ideology. However, when women's stories start to come from different feminist ethnographers from different perspectives, we reach closer to the truth through comparison and cross-checks. Feminist ethnographers collect their data from the oral history of women because their stories are not covered by historians and the State's policy makers. Saikia suggests that when traditional historiography ignores the truth about women's connection to any ethnic struggle, the oral history can be a vital source of the truth (2011b, 88–89). Narrative non-fiction is an integral part of human rights research, but the fabrication of these narratives has raised significant questions regarding its authenticity in representing the truth. After collecting information and seeking consent from people, these narratives face a careful manipulation of truth and emotion in the editorial process (Whitlock 2007, 3). In most cases, these interviews are oral narratives by individuals rather than a set of pre-existing historical narratives written by historians and scholars. One can surely question the reliability of oral history as it is contingent upon memory, which may fade or aggravate depending upon how much the bearer has retained and thought about it. Such an opinion is very subjective and, therefore, cannot be held the same for all individuals. Oral history can be a vital weapon for decoding the truth in human subject research, provided it is impersonal. Both autobiographies and oral testimonies play pertinent roles in human subject research, but unlike autobiographies, oral history explores the issues in common people's lives (Chamberlain and Thompson 1998, 4). The social and human rights discourses are also influenced by oral narratives because '[w]e are born into webs of narrative: micro-narratives of familial life and macro narratives of collective identity, codes of established narratives that define our capacities to weave individual life stories' (Whitlock 2007, 11). These narratives cannot be claimed as factual because narratives in most cases are afflicted by trauma, distortion and fragmentation. Individual memory cannot represent events linearly. Though these narratives can reveal the truth differently, they can change a set of memories, and new narratives may evolve from these (Saikia 2011b, 90). In this regard, the recent cases of Rigoberta Menchú and Binjamin Wilkomirski are noteworthy to show the existence of the fabrication of truth in narrative non-fiction. Menchú, a Nobel laureate, described the slaughter of her family members and several other Mayan Indians by the Guatemalan army in her autobiographical narrative non-fiction, *I, Rigoberta Menchú: An Indian woman in Guatemala* (1984). Binjamin Wilkomirski claimed to be one of the child survivors of a

Nazi camp and recorded his narrative of suffering, oppression and victimisation of his fellow companions during the Holocaust in his narrative non-fiction *Fragments from a Childhood* (1996). However, both their stories of survival as victims appeared to be fabricated partially or fully, as they lived outside these conflicted areas during the genocide (Peskin 2000, 39). The testimonies of victims play an important role in locating the truth behind genocide because we, as people, always expect a victim's account to be unbiased and true. Such references, however, question the integrity of the author and the authenticity of the victims' narratives. The number of martyrs and rape victims may have been fabricated in the narratives by both sides. The common estimate of three million deaths and two to four million rape victims (Linton 2010b; Sundar and Sundar 2014) is allegedly falsified, according to Bose (2011a) and other Pakistani writers. However, most ethnographic works (Mookherjee 2015b; D'Costa 2011) and feature articles (Zakaria 2019; Zaman 2020; Qasmi 2017) support Bangladesh's claims that the intensity of genocide and gender violence by the Pakistani army was extreme.

The Trajectories of Women's Narratives

The connection between feminist ethnographic works of the Liberation War of Bangladesh and its reality can only be assumed while studying Bangladesh's present development in human resource index and women's empowerment along with the recognition of the Birangona and Bihari victims. Bangladesh has started to acknowledge its women's contribution to the 1971 war that created the nation. The emergence of subaltern voices through their oral narratives as brought to the fore by several ethnographers and writers has helped the Bangladesh government to take major decisions in the judicial process of war criminals accused of gender crimes in the 1971 war. An important instance of the recognition of victims' narratives is Bangladesh's recent trials of war criminals in which the voices of these rape survivors played a major role. Both the fictional and non-fictional works selected in this book have been helpful to reread the traditional historiography of Bangladesh from a feminist perspective. A postmodern approach to ethnography inspires the inclusion of the accounts of the conflict in non-fiction, but ethnographic fiction is equally helpful. At the same time, both are prone to fabrication.

The postmodern approach to qualitative research is purely interdisciplinary and blurs the genres of its previous phase. A writer of this age 'creates narratives, braided compositions woven into and through field experiences' (Denzin and Lincoln 2018, 60). Postmodern ethnography, especially feminist ethnography, is also braided with narratives retrieved from oral history for the reconstruction of history and public consciousness regarding unknown or politically misrepresented facts. The crucial question is whether we are ready to accept the genuine history or we prefer a fabricated masculine version of it. The answer is not easy. The gradual emergence of oral history, mostly by women, due to the hard work of contemporary activists and anthropologists undoubtedly creates public consciousness. However, a majority of the population still prefers to believe in that masculine version of history where women are presented only as victims and outsiders without any skills to contribute. The tendency to suppress their voices is still present, and raped women face ostracisation for making their voices public. The love story between a rape victim and a Pakistani soldier is considered detrimental to Bangladesh's image, and the depiction of such events in literature or films faces public rejection and uproar. Rubaiyat Hossain's *Meherjaan* (2011), produced by A. Mostafa, is an award-winning film that was banned in Bangladeshi theatres for its portrayal of the love affair between a Baloch soldier and a Bengali woman during the 1971 war. When the people are unable to tolerate cinematic representation, how will the real story of Ferdousi Priyabhashini's falling in love with a Pakistani soldier get a place as a love story during the struggle? Interestingly, Ferdousi Priyabhashini, who confessed her love for a Pakistani soldier to Saikia (2011b), appears to be very critical of this film. According to her, the depiction of such a love affair undermines the sacrifice of the rape victims of the war like her (Ethirajan 2011). So, the point is that a majority of the people are still intolerant and do not want to accept the truth in many cases, whether it is related to rapes, war crimes, genocide, fabrication or love in moments of crisis. On the other hand, many people are interested in knowing the truth, conducting a sincere investigation and accepting the voices of the women. Women's stories of the 1971 war reveal many bitter truths that might offend traditional patriarchal and nationalistic ideologies.

This book is based on the feminist narratives of the 1971 war that give a fresh perspective to the studies of women's roles in the war and their plights in the post-war context of Bangladesh based on their representation in contemporary ethnographic fiction and non-fiction. As this book has focused on multiple novels and non-fictional works, several perspectives were presented such as women's engagement in nationalist politics, their involvement in the war as fighters and social workers and their deplorable condition as victims. However, the issues found here cannot be declared absolute because the postmodern approach to feminism as well as ethnography does not believe in absolute knowledge and does not privilege any specific approach. Richardson and Pierre say, 'A postmodernist position does allow us to know "something" without claiming to know everything' (2018, 1413). Feminist ethnography also advocates such relativism over homogenised issues regarding truths and their representation. When the traditional mode of feminism was accused of being racist and homogenised, anthropologists resolved the issue with their approach to cultural relativism for the sake of a heterogenised and context-specific lens to evaluate women's issues (Visweswaran 1994, 20). We have tried to focus on many accumulated 'somethings' about women's issues, their involvement in the 1971 war, their victimisation and their post-war condition based on multiple perspectives of feminist ethnographic interpretation of professional anthropologists and women activists. This book leaves space for speculation over the issues discussed here because the postmodern approach to feminist ethnography accommodates several voices on a single issue but never claims to settle the truth (Aune 2009, 313). The writers have accommodated several voices on the single issues of women and/in the 1971 war to get multiple perspectives. To ensure objectivity, all the claims made by the writers and ethnographers have been evaluated with references from secondary sources. Many issues like women's victimisation in ethnic politics, their agency in the war and their post-war position as Birangona and Bihari women were found appropriate with very few contradictions. A few issues appear contradictory and fabricated such as the downplaying of the number of victims and the ethnic politics behind the victimisation of Hindu women and Bihari women. So, more engagement is needed to get a detailed picture of women and their association with the ethnic conflict. Focusing on the lived experience of women of the 1971 war will surely motivate people to begin the process of exploring war memories based on shared memories in Bangladesh and beyond (Saikia 2011b, 242). The shared memories of women as presented in women's ethnographic literature of the 1971 war broadens the insights for future researchers to break the silence and reframe public consciousness about the actual contribution women made in the conflict. Bangladesh celebrated fifty years of independence in 2021. Hence, this book is likely to be a noteworthy contribution to their studies of the history of the 1971 war.

References

Ahmad, R.B. 2016. 'A Political History of Bangladesh.' *Daily Star*, 27 November 2016. Accessed 5 November 2017. http://www.thedailystar.net/book-reviews/political-history-bangladesh-1321318.

Ahsan, S.B. 2012. 'Review of *Dead Reckoning: Memories of the 1971 Bangladesh War* and *Women, War and the Making of Bangladesh*.' *Asian Affairs* 43 (3): 505–507. DOI: 10.1080/03068374.2012.720775.

Akhtar, S. 2006. *Taalash*. Dhaka: Mowla Brothers.

Amin, A.M., L.A. Ahmed, and S. Ahsan. 2016. 'The Women in Our Liberation War.' *Daily Star*, 20 December 2016. Accessed 3 October 2018. https://www.thedailystar.net/supplements/victory-day-2016-special/the-women-our-liberation-war-1330396.

Anam, T. 2007. *A Golden Age*. London: John Murray.

———. 2008. 'The War that Time Forgot.' *Guardian*, 10 April. Accessed 17 June 2022. https://www.theguardian.com/world/2008/apr/10/bangladesh.photography.

———. 2011. *The Good Muslim*. New Delhi: Penguin.

Andrio, D. 2016. 'India's Role in the Emergence of Bangladesh as an Independent State.' *Vestnik Rudn International Relations* 16 (4): 736–744. DOI: 10.22363/2313-0660-2016-16-4-736-744.

Ara, D.Z. 2015. *Blame*. Dhaka: University Press Ltd Bangladesh.

Arif, M.K. 2015. 'Legal Status of Bihari Community.' *Daily Star*, 9 November 2015. Accessed 25 January 2019. https://www.thedailystar.net/law-our-rights/rights-advocacy/legal-status-bihari-community-169906.

Armitstead, C. 2016. 'Tahmima Anam: "I have a complicated relationship with Bangladesh".' *Guardian,* 13 May 2016. Accessed 17 November 2017. https://www.theguardian.com/books/2016/may/13/tahmima-anam-i-have-complicated-relationship-with-bangladesh-interview.

Ashe, L., and I. Patterson. 2014. *War and Literature*. Cambridge: D.S. Brewer.

Aune, K. 2009. 'Feminist Ethnography.' In *Encyclopedia of Gender and Society*, edited by J. O'Brien, 309–311. Thousand Oaks, CA: SAGE Publications, Inc. DOI: 10.4135/9781412964517.n159.

Baloch, S. 2017. 'The Woes of Bengalis, Burmese and Iranians of Karachi.' *Herald*, 14 September 2017. Accessed 18 February 2018. https://herald.dawn.com/news/1153771.

Banton, C. 2020. 'The Meaning of the Term Third World.' Investopedia, 5 February 2020. Accessed 20 November 2020. https://www.investopedia.com/terms/t/third-world.asp.

Barbre, J.W., and The Personal Narratives Group, eds. 1989. *Interpreting Women's Lives: Feminist Theory and Personal Narratives*. Bloomington: Indiana University Press.

Bass, G.J. 2012. *The Blood Telegram: India's Secret War in East Pakistan*. Noida: Random House India.

Biswas, S.K., and P. Tripathi. 2017. 'Relocating Women's Role in War: Rereading Tahmima Anam's A Golden Age.' *The Criterion: An International Journal in English* 8 (1): 522–528. Accessed 10 June 2018. http://www.the-criterion.com/V8/n1/070.pdf.

Boissoneault, L. 2016. 'The Genocide the U.S. Can't Remember, But Bangladesh Can't Forget.' *Smithsonian*, 16 December 2016. Accessed 16 December 2017. https://www.smithsonianmag.com/history/genocide-us-cant-remember-bangladesh-cant-forget-180961490/.

Bolla, P.D., H. White, and D. LaCapra. 1986. 'Disfiguring History.' *Diacritics* 16 (4): 48. DOI: 10.2307/464801.

Bose, S. 2007. 'Losing the Victims: Problems of Using Women as Weapons in Recounting the Bangladesh War.' *Economic and Political Weekly* 42 (38): 3864–3871. Accessed 21 July 2019. https://epw.in/journal/2007/38/special-articles/losing-victims-problems-using-women-weapons-recounting-bangladesh.

———. 2011a. *Dead Reckoning: Memories of the 1971 Bangladesh War*. C Hurst & Company.

———. 2011b. 'The Question of Genocide and the Quest for Justice in the 1971 War.' *Journal of Genocide Research* 13 (4): 393–419. DOI: 10.1080/14623528.2011.625750.

Brüggemeier, F.J. 1986. 'Sound of Silence: History, Narrative, and Life-Recollections.' *Poetics* 15: 5–24. DOI: 2010.1016_0304-422x(86)90029-x.

Burton-Hill, C. 2007. 'Review: *A Golden Age* by Tahmima Anam.' *Guardian*, 21 April 2007. Accessed 27 November 2020. https://www.theguardian.com/books/2007/apr/22/fiction.features.

Carter, D. 2014. 'Srinath Raghavan. 1971: A Global History of the Creation of Bangladesh; Gary J. Bass. The Blood Telegram: Nixon, Kissinger and a Forgotten Genocide.' *Asian Affairs* 45 (3): 519–521. DOI: 10.1080/03068374.2014.954220.

Cecconi, G. 2019. 'Stranded in Geneva Camp.' *Himal*, 27 June 2019. Accessed 23 January 2020. https://www.himalmag.com/geneva-camp-bihari-bangladesh-gabriele-cecconi-2019/.

Chamberlain, M., and P. Thompson. 1998. *Narrative and Genre*. London: Routledge.

Chatterjee, A. 2017. 'Remembering Bangladesh: Tahmima Anam and the Recuperation of a Bangladeshi National Narrative in Diaspora'. *South Asian Review* 35 (3): 131–148. DOI: 10.1080/02759527.2014.11932991.

Chodos, A., ed. 2006. 'This Month in Physics History: June, ca. 240 B.C. Eratosthenes Measures the Earth.' *APS Physics* 15 (6). Accessed 10 December 2019. https://www.aps.org/publications/apsnews/200606/history.cfm.

Cock, L. de. 1992. 'Interview with Gayatri Chakravorty Spivak: New Nation Writers Conference in South Africa.' *Ariel: A Review of International English* 23 (3): 29–47. Accessed 21 July 2019. https://web.archive.org/web/20110706205400/http://ariel.synergiesprairies.ca/ariel/index.php/ariel/article/viewFile/2505/2458.

Cook, B.A. 2006. *Women and War: A Historical Encyclopedia from Antiquity to the Present*. Santa Barbara, CA: ABC-Clio.

D'Costa, B. 2011. *Nationbuilding, Gender and War Crimes in South Asia*. London: Routledge.

———. 2012. 'Review of *Women, War, and the Making of Bangladesh: Remembering 1971*.' *Journal of Genocide Research* 14 (1): 110–114. DOI: 10.1080/14623528.2012.656994.

Daily Star. 2008. 'A Photographer Looks Back at 1971.' 1 December 2008. Accessed 17 June 2022. https://www.thedailystar.net/news-detail-65606.

Das, B., and S. Berning. 2011. 'Rape Victims or War Heroes: War Women in Bangladesh.' DW, 28 June 2011. Accessed 26 August 2020. https://www.dw.com/en/rape-victims-or-war-heroes-war-women-in-bangladesh/a-6556207.

Das, C. 2013. 'Book Review: Sarmila Bose. *Dead Reckoning: Memories of the 1971 Bangladesh War*.' *Journal of South Asian Development* 8 (1): 136–138. DOI: 10.1177/0973174113477014.

Das, C. 2017. *In the Land of Buried Tongues: Testimonies and Literary Narratives of the War of Liberation War of Bangladesh*. New Delhi: Oxford University Press.

Davis, Dána-Ain, and C. Craven. 2016. *Feminist Ethnography: Thinking through Methodologies, Challenges, and Possibilities*. Lanham, MD: Rowman & Littlefield Publishers.

Denzin, N.K., and Y.S. Lincoln. 2018. 'Introduction: The Discipline and Practice of Qualitative Research.' In *The SAGE Handbook of Qualitative Research*, edited by N.K. Denzin and Y.S. Lincoln, 29–71. London: SAGE Publications Ltd.

Dummett, M. 2011. 'Bangladesh War: The Article that Changed History.' BBC, 16 December 2011. Accessed 8 August 2020. http://www.bbc.com/news/world-asia-16207201.

Ethirajan, A. 2011. 'Bangladeshi War Film Meherjaan Rekindles Old Enmities.' BBC, 11 April 2011. Accessed 17 December 2018. http://www.bbc.co.uk/news/mobile/world-south-asia-13034953.

Gakhar, R. 2018. 'What does Schools of Pakistan Teach about 1971 War?' Defence Lover, 28 February 2018. Accessed 26 July 2019. https://defencelover.in/what-does-schools-of-pakistan-teach-about-1971-war/.

Ganguly, S. 2016. 'Srinath Raghavan, 1971: A Global History of the Creation of Bangladesh'. *Journal of Cold War Studies* 18 (3): 194–195. DOI: 10.1162/jcws_r_00660

Gazdar, H. 2003. *A Review of Migration Issues in Pakistan*. Accessed 21 June 2020. http://www.researchcollective.org/Documents/A_Review_of_Migration_Issues_in_Pakistan.pdf.

Ghosh, A. 2011. *The Shadow Lines*. London: John Murray.

Ghosh, S. 2016. 'Feminist Ethnography.' In *The Wiley Blackwell Encyclopedia of Gender and Sexuality Studies*, edited by A. Wong, M. Wickramasinghe, R. Hoogland and N.A. Naples, 1–9. New Jersey: John Wiley & Sons. DOI: 10.1002/9781118663219.wbegss765.

Gramuglia, P.M. 2009. 'Unsettling Accounts: Neither Truth nor Reconciliation in Confessions of State Violence—by Payne, Leigh A.' *Bulletin of Latin American Research* 28 (1): 150–151. DOI: 10.1111/j.1470-9856.2008.0293_17.x.

Grimaldo, J. 2017. 'Why has Sisterhood Failed to Organize Women against Oppression?' Medium, 23 March 2017. Accessed 2 June 2018. https://

medium.com/@HelloCherubs/why-has-sisterhood-failed-to-organize-women-against-oppression-3c7fd628271c.

Guhathakurta, B. 1991. *Ekattorer Smriti* [Memory of 71]. Dhaka: The University Press Limited.

Haider, Z. 2018. 'Biharis in Bangladesh and Their Restricted Access to Citizenship Rights.' *South Asia Research* 38 (3 suppl): 25S–42S. DOI: 10.1177/0262728018791695.

Hall, S. 1997. *Representation: Cultural Representation and Signifying Practices*. London: The Open University/SAGE.

Hannan, S.A. 2007. 'There was No Genocide; It was a "Civil War".' *Daily Star*, 27 October 2007. Accessed 5 May 2019. https://www.thedailystar.net/news-detail-9204.

Haque, J. 2016. 'Blame: A 1971 Novel.' *Dhaka Tribune,* 21 May 2016. Accessed 2 October 2017. http://archive.dhakatribune.com/arts-letters/2016/may/21/blame-1971-novel.

Hart, J. 2011. *Story Craft: The Complete Guide to Writing Narrative Nonfictions.* London: The University of Chicago Press Ltd.

Hasanat, F. 2017. 'Religion, Diaspora and the Politics of a Homing Desire in the Writings of Zia Haider Rahman, Tahmima Anam and Monica Ali.' *Asiatic: IIUM Journal of English Language and Literature* 11 (1): 57–68. Accessed 15 June 2018. https://journals.iium.edu.my/asiatic/index.php/AJELL/article/view/962/694.

Herbert, C. 2011. 'Lyric Maps and the Legacies of 1971 in Kamila Shamsie's Kartography.' *Journal of Postcolonial Writing* 47 (2): 159–172. DOI: 10.1080/17449855.2011.557188.

Homans, M. 1994. 'Feminist Fictions and Feminist Theories of Narrative.' *Narratives* 2 (1): 3–16. Accessed 20 November 2020. https://www.jstor.org/stable/20107020.

Hoque, A. 2012. *Freedom's Mother*. New Delhi: Palimpsest.

Hossain, A. 2012. '1971 Rapes: Bangladesh Cannot Hide History.' *Forbes*, 12 May 2012. Accessed 15 May 2019. https://www.forbes.com/sites/worldviews/2012/05/21/1971-rapes-bangladesh-cannot-hide-history/.

Hossain, R. 2011. '1971: Shall We Remember, Forget, or Fabricate?' Rubaiyat Hossain. 13 June 2011. Accessed 24 December 2018. https://rubaiyat-hossain.com/2011/06/09/1971-shall-we-remember-forget-or-fabricate/.

Hossain, R. dir. 2011. *Meherjaan.* [Motion Picture.] Bangladesh: Khona Talkies. Produced by A. Mostafa.

Huda, S. 2018. 'The Lonely Path that Rama Chowdhury Walked.' *Daily Star*, 6 September 2018. Accessed 16 December 2018. http://www.thedailystar.net/news/opinion/tribute/the-lonely-path-rama-chowdhury-walked-1629595.

Ibrahim, N. 1994. *Aami Birangana Balchi* [A war heroine, I speak]. Dhaka: Jagroti Prokashon.

———. 2017. *A War Heroine, I Speak.* Translated by F. Hasanat. Dhaka: Bangla Academy.

Imam, J. 1986. *Ekattorer Dinguli* [The days of 71]. Dhaka: Shandhani Prakashan.

Iqbal, M.Z. 2008. *Muktijuddher Itihas* [History of the freedom struggle]. Dhaka: Pratiti.

James, H. 1884. 'The Art of Fiction.' Virgil. Accessed 26 March 2020.http://virgil.org/dswo/courses/novel/james-fiction.pdf.

Karam, A. 2000. 'Women in War and Peace-building: The Roads Traversed, the Challenges Ahead.' *International Feminist Journal of Politics* 3 (1): 2–25. DOI: 10.1080/14616740010019820.

Karim, E. 2018. 'Tribute to Rama Chowdhury.' *Daily* Star, 3 September 2018. Accessed 16 December 2018. http://www.thedailystar.net/news/backpage/tribute-ekattorer-janani-1628776.

Kaufman, J.P. 2016. 'Women and Children, War and Peace: Political Agency in Time of Conflict.' *International Affairs* 92 (6): 1499–1504. DOI: 10.1111/1468-2346.12756.

Khan, S. 2004. *Noor*. New Delhi: Penguin Books India.

King, B. 2011. 'Kamila Shamsie's Novels of History, Exile and Desire.' *Journal of Postcolonial Writing* 47 (2): 147–158. DOI: 10.1080/17449855.2011.557186.

Kumar, R. 2001. 'Womens Peacekeeping During Ethnic Conflicts and Post-Conflict Reconstruction.' *NWSA Journal* 13 (2): 68–73. DOI: 10.2979/nws.2001.13.2.68.

Lambek, M. 2016. 'Review of Nayanika Mookherjee's *The Spectral Wound: Sexual Violence, Public Memories, and the Bangladesh War of 1971.*' *Journal of the Royal Anthropological Institute* 22 (4): 1001–1002. DOI: 10.1111/1467-9655.12517.

Lambert, R.D. 1959. 'Factors in Bengali Regionalism in Pakistan.' *Far Eastern Survey* 28 (4): 49–58. DOI: 10.1525/as.1959.28.4.01p1259x.

Lee, J. 1997. 'Women Re-authoring their Lives through Feminist Narrative Therapy.' *Women & Therapy* 20 (3): 1–22. DOI: 10.1300/j015v20n03_01.

Lezard, N. 2003. 'Review: *Kartography* by Kamila Shamsie.' *Guardian*, 7 June 2003. Accessed 5 October 2020. http://www.theguardian.com/books/2003/jun/07/featuresreviews.guardianreview2.

Linton, S. 2010a. 'Bangladesh and the Prosecution of International Crimes from the 1971 War of Independence from Pakistan.' *Criminal Law Forum* 21 (2): 187–190. DOI: 10.1007/s10609-010-9121-1.

———. 2010b. 'Completing the Circle: Accountability for the Crimes of the 1971 Bangladesh War of Liberation.' *Criminal Law Forum* 21 (2): 191–311. DOI: 10.1007/s10609-010-9121-1.

Malik, I. 2008. *The History of Pakistan*. California: Greenwood.

Malle, B.F., S. Guglielmo, and A.E. Monroe. 2014. 'A Theory of Blame.' *Psychological Inquiry* 25 (2): 147–186. DOI: 10.1080/1047840x.2014.877340.

Mamoon, M. 2017. *Birangana 1971: Saga of the Violated Women*. Dhaka: Journeyman Books.

Masud, T., and C. Masud, dirs. 1999. *Muktir Kotha.* [Motion Picture]. Bangladesh: Audiovision.

McDermott, R.F. 2012. 'A History of Bangladesh.' *Journal of Asian Studies* 71 (1): 294–296. DOI: 10.1017/s0021911811002865.

McFadden, C. 2014. 'Incarcerated Women: Victimhood, Empowerment, and Resistance in Prison.' Paper presented at the Michigan Sociological Association Conference, Muskegon, Michigan, 25 December 2014.

Meintjes, S. 2000. 'Introduction: The Aftermath: Women in Post-War Reconstruction.' *Agenda* 43 (4): 4–10. DOI: 10.2307/4066104

———. 2011. 'The Aftermath: Women in Post-War Reconstruction.' *Agenda* 16 (3): 4–10. DOI: 10.2307/4066104.

Meister, R. 2012. 'Human Rights and the Politics of Victimhood.' *Ethics & International Affairs* 16 (2): 91–108. DOI: 10.1111/j.1747-7093.2002.tb00400.x.

Menchú, R., and E. Burgos-Debray. 1984. *I, Rigoberta Menchú: An Indian Woman in Guatemala*. London: Verso.

Mitra, R. 2012. 'A Traveler's Guide to Dhaka, Bangladesh.' *Call to Humanity: Rahul Mitra's Blog*, 6 April 2014. Accessed 27 May 2018. Retrieved from https://calltohumanity.wordpress.com/tag/bangladesh/.

Mohaiemen, N. 2012. 'Prisoners of Shothik Itihash.' New Age BD, 31 March 2014. Accessed 6 May 2019. http://www.newagebd.com/detail.php?date=2012-03-31&nid=5208#.UqkxV41Q2wI.

Mohanty, C.T. 1984. 'Under Western Eyes: Feminist Scholarship and Colonial Discourses.' *Boundary* 12 (3): 333–358.

———. 2003. *Feminism without Borders: Decolonizing Theory, Practicing Solidarity*. Durham: Duke University Press.

Mohua, M., and M.T. Mowtushi. 2019. 'Bangladesh.' *The Journal of Commonwealth Literature* 54 (4): 533–549. DOI: 10.1177/0021989419877045.

Mollah, M.A. 2019. 'War Crimes Trials in Bangladesh: Justice or Politics?' *Journal of Asian and African Studies* 55 (5): 652–665. DOI: 10.1177/0021909619890117.

Mookherjee, N. 2006. 'Remembering to Forget: Public Secrecy and Memory of Sexual Violence in the Bangladesh War of 1971.' *Journal of the Royal Anthropological Institute* 12 (2): 433–450. DOI: 10.1111/j.1467-9655.2006.00299.x.

———. 2011. 'This Account of the Bangladesh War Should Not be Seen as Unbiased.' *Guardian,* 8 June 2011. Accessed 14 July 2018. https://www.theguardian.com/commentisfree/2011/jun/08/bangladesh-liberation-war-sarmila-bose.

———. 2015a. 'The Raped Woman as a Horrific Sublime and the Bangladesh War of 1971.' *Journal of Material Culture* 20 (4): 379–395. DOI: 10.1177/1359183515603742

———. 2015b. *The Spectral Wound: Sexual Violence, Public Memories, and the Bangladesh War of 1971*. London: Duke University Press.

Mortuza, S. 2016. 'Whose Blame Is It Anyway?' *Daily Star,* 7 February 2016. www.thedailystar.net/book-reviews/whose-blame-it-anyway-214261.

Muecke, M.A. 1994. 'On the Evaluation of Ethnographies.' In *Critical Issues in Qualitative Research Methods*, edited by J.M. Morse, 187–209. New York: SAGE Publications Ltd.

Mughal, B.K., and S. Baloch. 2017. 'The Woes of Bengalis, Burmese and Iranians of Karachi.' *Herald*, 14 September 2017. Accessed 19 July 2019. https://herald.dawn.com/news/1153771.

Murshed, T.M. 1997. 'Women, Islam and the State in Bangladesh: Subordination and Resistance.' Swadhinata. Accessed 26 July 2017. https://swadhinata.org.uk/wp-content/uploads/2017/08/WomenBdeshTazeen.pdf.

Nanda, S.M. 2018. 'Challenges for Women's Peace activism in South Asia.' In *Women, Conflict and Peace Processes in South Asia* [pamphlet], Benaras Hindu University, 21–22 November 2018.

Navarro-Tejero, A. 2019. 'Sacks of Mutilated Breasts: Violence and Body Politics in South Asian Partition Literature.' *Journal of International Women's Studies* 20 (3): 44–50. Accessed 20 March 2020. https://vc.bridgew.edu/jiws/vol20/iss3/5.

Nayar, P.K. 2016. *Human Rights and Literature.* New York: Palgrave Macmillan.

Parashar, S. 2018. 'The WPS Agenda: A Postcolonial Agenda.' In *The Oxford Handbook of Women, Peace, and Security,* edited by Sara E. Davies and Jacqui True, 828–839. New York: Oxford University Press. DOI: 10.1093/oxfordhb/9780190638276.013.46.

Peskin, H. 2000. 'Memory and Media: "Cases" of Rigoberta Menchú and Binjamin Wilkomirski.' *Society* 38 (1): 39–46. DOI: 10.1007/s12115-000-1005-2.

Portelli, A. 1998. 'Oral History as Genre.' In *Narrative and Genre*, 23–45. London: Routledge.

Ptacek, J. 2016. 'Rape and the Continuum of Sexual Abuse in Intimate Relationships.' In *Marital Rape: Consent, Marriage and Social Change in Global Context*, edited by K. Yllö and M.G. Torres. New York: Oxford University Press.

Purushothaman, U. 2012. 'Book Review: Gary J. Bass, *The Blood Telegram: India's Secret War in Pakistan.*' *International Studies* 49 (3–4): 461–463. DOI: 10.1177/0020881714534548.

Qasmi, A.U. 2017. '1971 War: Witness to History.' *Herald*, 17 February 2017. Accessed 25 January 2019. https://herald.dawn.com/news/1153304.

Qazi, F. 2016. *Secrets of the Kashmir Valley: My Journey through the Conflict between India and Pakistan*. New Delhi: Pharos.

Raghavan, S. 2013. *1971: A Global History of the Creation of Bangladesh*. Cambridge, MA: Harvard University Press.

Rahman, B. 2018. 'Language Movement: A History Written in Blood.' *Daily Sun*, 20 February 2018. Accessed 20 April 2020. https://www.daily-sun.com/post/290312/2018/02/20/Language-Movement:-A-History-Written-in-Blood.

Rahman, H.H. (1982) 2009. *Bangladesher Shadhinota Juddha: Dolilpotro*. Dhaka: Hakkani Publishers on behalf of the Government of the Peoples Republic of Bangladesh.

Ranjan, A. 2016. 'Bangladesh Liberation War of 1971: Narratives, Impacts and the Actors.' *India Quarterly: A Journal of International Affairs* 72 (2): 132–145. DOI: 10.1177/0974928416637921.

Report, S.O. 2018. 'Geneva Camp in Dhaka's Muhammadpur.' *Daily Star,* 26 May 2018. Accessed 26 January 2019. https://www.thedailystar.net/city/geneva-camp-dhakas-muhammadpur-1581955.

Richardson, L. 2000. 'Evaluating Ethnography.' *Qualitative Inquiry* 6 (2): 253–255. DOI: 10.1177/107780040000600207.

Richardson, L., and E.A. Pierre. 2018. 'Writing: A Method of Inquiry.' In *The SAGE Handbook of Qualitative Research, 5th Edition,* edited by N.K. Denzin and Y.S. Lincoln, 1410–1422. London: SAGE Publications Ltd.

Roy, M.S. 2019. 'The Women of 1971: On Either Side of the Bengal Border.' *Wire,* 19 February 2019. Accessed 2 April 2019. https://thewire.in/women/1971-bengal-violence-women-naxalbari.

Rozario, R.R., and S. Uttom. 2019. 'Bangladesh: Violence Highlights Plight of Bangladesh's Bihari Muslims.' *South Asia Journal,* 11 October 2019. Accessed 2 February 2020. http://southasiajournal.net/bangladesh-violence-highlights-plight-of-bangladeshs-bihari-muslims/.

Rushdie, S. (1981) 2013. *Midnight's Children*. London: Vintage.

———. (1983) 2008. *Shame*. New York: Random House Trade Paperbacks.

Sadkar, M.P. n.d. 'Why Women's History?' National Women's History Alliance. Accessed 26 January 2019. https://nationalwomenshistoryalliance.org/why-womens-history/.

Saikia, Y. 2004. 'Beyond the Archive of Silence: Narratives of Violence of the 1971 Liberation War of Bangladesh.' *History Workshop Journal* 58 (1): 275–287. DOI: 10.1093/hwj/58.1.275.

———. 2011a. 'Insāniyat for Peace: Survivors Narrative of the 1971 War of Bangladesh.' *Journal of Genocide Research* 13 (4): 475–501. DOI: 10.1080/14623528.2011.625739.

———. 2011b. *Women, War, and the Making of Bangladesh: Remembering 1971*. Durham: Duke University Press.

Schendel, W.V. 2009. *A History of Bangladesh*. Cambridge: Cambridge University Press.

Shamsie, K. 2002. *Kartography*. London: Bloomsbury.

———. 2010. 'Kamila Shamsie on Leaving and Returning to Karachi.' *Guardian,* 13 March 2010. Accessed 24 December 2018. https://www.theguardian.com/books/2010/mar/13/karachi-leaving-london-writing-fiction.

Shoemaker, J. 2002. 'In War and Peace: Women and Conflict Prevention.' *Civil Wars* 5 (1): 27–54. DOI: 10.1080/13698240208402494.

Singh, A. 2008. 'Review: Tahmima Anam's *A Golden Age*.' Lehigh, 7 March 2008. Accessed 3 April 2020. https://www.lehigh.edu/~amsp/2008/03/review-tahmima-anams-golden-age.html.

Sisson, R., and L.E. Rose. 1992. *War and Secession: Pakistan, India, and the Creation of Bangladesh*. California: University of California Press.

Smith, S. 2011. 'Narrating Lives.' *Profession* 1: 5–12. DOI: 10.1632/prof.2011.2011.1.5.

Snow, N.E. 1994. 'Self-Blame and Blame of Rape Victims.' *Public Affairs Quarterly* 8.4 (October): 377–393.

Spivak, G.C. 1988. *Can the Subaltern Speak?* Basingstoke: Macmillan.

Sun, T.D. 2019. '25th Death anniversary of Jahanara Imam Today.' *Daily Sun*, 25 June 2019. Accessed 6 July 2020. https://www.daily-sun.com/post/402194/2019/06/25/25th-death-anniversary-of-Jahanara-Imam-today.

Sundar, A., and N. Sundar. 2014. *Civil Wars in South Asia: State, Sovereignty, Development*. New Delhi: SAGE Publications Ltd.

Throop, S.A. 2014. 'Acts of Vengeance, Acts of Love: Crusading Violence in the Twelfth Century.' In *War and Literature*, edited by L. Ashe and I. Patterson, 3–20. Cambridge: D.S. Brewer.

Townsend, M. 2017. 'Bangladesh: The Forgotten Genocide.' College of Arts and Sciences. 26 April 2017. Accessed 15 May 2019. https://cas.uab.edu/humanrights/2017/04/21/bangladesh-forgotten-genocide/.

UNICEF (United Nations Children's Fund). n.d. 'Sexual Violence as a Weapon of War.' UNICEF. Accessed 2 May 2018. http://www.unicef.org/sowc96pk/sexviol.htm.

Visweswaran, K. 1994. *Fictions of Feminist Ethnography*. Minneapolis: University of Minnesota Press.

Wakelin, A., and K.M. Long. 2003. 'Effects of Victim Gender and Sexuality on Attributions of Blame to Rape Victims.' *Sex Roles* 49 (9/10): 477–487. DOI: 10.1023/a:1025876522024.

Waterman, D. 2015. 'Kamila Shamsie's Kartography and the Itinerary of Cultural Identity.' *Sillages Critiques* 19. Accessed 20 December 2019. https://journals.openedition.org/sillagescritiques/4295?lang=en#quotation.

Watts, C. 2014. 'Unnavigable Kinship in a Time of Conflict: Loyalist Calligraphies, Sovereign Power and the "Muckle Honor" of Elizabeth Murray Inman.' In *War and Literature*, edited by L. Ashe and I. Patterson, 139–162. Cambridge: D.S. Brewer.

White, H. 1980. 'The Value of Narrativity in the Representation of Reality.' *Critical Inquiry* 7 (1): 5–27. DOI: 10.1086/448086.

Whitlock, G. 2007. *Soft Weapons: Autobiography in Transit.* Chicago: Chicago University Press.

Wilkomirski, B. 1996. *Fragments from a Childhood, 1939–1945.* London: Picador.

Woolf, V. 1929. *A Room of One's Own*. London: The Hogarth Press. Reprinted by HarperCollins in 1977.

Wright, T. 2013. 'Tahmima Anam.' British Council, January 2013. Accessed 31 December 2019. https://literature.britishcouncil.org/writer/tahmima-anam.

Yllö, K., and M.G. Torres, eds. 2016. *Marital Rape: Consent, Marriage, and Social Change in the Global Context.* New York, NY: Oxford University Press.

Zakaria, A. 2019. 'Remembering the War of 1971 in East Pakistan.' *Al Jazeera*, 16 December 2019. Accessed 10 February 2020. https://www.aljazeera.com/indepth/opinion/remembering-war-1971-east-pakistan-191216054546348.html

Zaman, R. 2011. *Invisible lines*. New York: HarperCollins.

Zaman, S. 2020. 'We Mistreated, Exploited and Massacred Bangladeshis: Pakistani Scientist.' *TBS*, 16 February 2020. Accessed 21 February 2020. https://tbsnews.net/opinion/we-mistreated-exploited-and-massacred-bangladeshis-pakistani-scientist-45127.

Zwier, D. 2018. 'Bangladesh War Crimes Tribunal Sentences 5 to Death for 1971 Crimes.' Jurist. 14 August 2018. Accessed 21 February 2020. https://www.jurist.org/news/2018/08/bangladesh-war-crimes-tribunal-sentences-5-to-death-for-1971-crimes/.

Index

About the Authors

Sanjib Kr Biswas presently works as a postgraduate teacher of English at Rasakhowa High School (HS), West Bengal. Formerly, he served as an academic counsellor of English at Indira Gandhi National Open University. He completed his PhD in 2021 from the Department of Humanities and Social Sciences, Indian Institute of Technology Patna. He is the recipient of two state-level prizes for writing. He has been published in journals such as *Asiatic: IIUM Journal of English Language and Literature*, *Journal of International Women's Studies* (Bridgewater State University, Massachusetts) and *Journal of Gender Studies* (Taylor & Francis). His book chapter was featured in *Bangladeshi Literature in English: A Critical Anthology* (2021, Asiatic Society of Bangladesh). He can be reached at sanjib.phs16@iitp.ac.in. His ORCID id is https://orcid.org/0000-0002-9351-489X.

Priyanka Tripathi is an associate professor of English and head of the Department of Humanities and Social Sciences at the Indian Institute of Technology Patna. She is the co-executive editor of the *Journal of International Women's Studies* (JIWS). She has been awarded a visiting research fellowship (2022–2023), by the Institute for Advanced Studies in the Humanities at the University of Edinburgh, Edinburgh, for her project titled 'Optimizing Caste Intersectionality: A Decolonial Reading of Gender-based Violence in Select Subaltern Fiction in India'. She has published extensively in *Indian Literature, Journal of Graphic Novels and Comics, GeoHumanities* and *Economic and Political Weekly* amongst others. She has received several grants, such as the JIWS fellowship 2021–2022 (Bridgewater State University, Massachusetts), the Shastri Conference and Lecture Series Grant (SCLSG) 2021–2022, the Post-colonial Association grant 2020–2021 and the Central Institute of Indian Languages (CIIL) conference grant 2020 amongst others. She has also worked on several government-sponsored projects related to gender issues. She works in the area of gender studies, South Asian fiction, GeoHumanities and graphic novels. Her email address is priyankatripathi@iitp.ac.in and ORCID id is https://orcid.org/0000-0002-9522.